CAMBRIDGE MUSIC HANDBOOKS

Beethoven: Symphony No. 9

CAMBRIDGE MUSIC HANDBOOKS

GENERAL EDITOR Julian Rushton

Recent titles

Beethoven: Symphony No. 9

Nicholas Cook

Professor of Music, University of Southampton

Published by the Press Syndicate of the University of Cambridge
The Pitt Building, Trumpington Street, Cambridge CB2 1RP
40 West 20th Street, New York, NY 10011–4211, USA
10 Stamford Road, Oakleigh, Melbourne 3166, Australia

First published 1993
Reprinted 1996, 1999

Printed in the United Kingdom at the University Press, Cambridge

A cataloguing in publication record for this book is available from the British Library

Library of Congress cataloguing in publication data

Cook, Nicholas, 1950–
Beethoven: Symphony No. 9 / Nicholas Cook
p. cm. – (Cambridge music handbooks)
Includes bibliographical references and index.
ISBN 0 521 39039 7 (hardback) – ISBN 0 521 39924 6 (paperback)
1. Beethoven, Ludwig van, 1770–1827. Symphony No. 9, op. 125, D minor.
I. Title. II. Series.
ML410.B42C66 1993
784.2'184–dc20 92–20451 CIP MN

ISBN 0 521 39039 7 hardback
ISBN 0 521 39924 6 paperback

AH

Contents

Contents

Preface

'A fog of verbiage and criticism surrounds the *Choral Symphony*', wrote Claude-Achille Debussy; 'It is amazing that it has not been finally buried under the mass of prose which it has provoked.'[1] Disquieting words indeed for the author of a new handbook! But it is worth examining what Debussy is saying. He is approaching the Ninth Symphony rather as if it were an archaeological site; he implies that we need to dig away the debris of more recent times in order to uncover the work as Beethoven created it. Or we might liken the symphony to a painting, revealed in its original colours when the accretions and encrustations of later ages have been stripped off. In either case, the aim is to get back to the original. And this has been the guiding principle of most twentieth-century musicology; the performance practice movement is merely the most conspicuous example of such historical reconstruction, the aim of which is to reveal the music as its composer intended it. But, in the case of the Ninth Symphony, is erasing the accretions of history the most profitable way to approach the music? Is it even possible?

'This Symphony', wrote F. J. Crowest in 1899, 'has that infinite sublimity and dramatic power, that sympathy with humanity which make it the most wonderful musical revelation that could be desired, or that is ever likely to be devised.' So far, so good. But then Crowest adds:

What it was all intended to convey the world knows not, at least, not from Beethoven. No programme of the music ever escaped its composer. . . . Some call it a 'monstrous madness'; some, 'the last flickers of an expiring genius'; others hope to understand and appreciate it one day. . . . The world, therefore, must build up its own conclusions.[2]

And the sense of perplexity that lies behind Crowest's words was shared by many earlier listeners. The Ninth Symphony seemed to go out of its way to flout established conventions. It was so difficult as to be almost impossible to perform, and so long as to be almost impossible to programme. It introduced voices into the symphony, words into the flagship genre of absolute music. It lurched from the sublime to the farcical and back again, counterpointing the 'Turkish' music of contemporary street entertainment with the most strict and elaborate fugal techniques.

If the Ninth Symphony had been written not by Beethoven but by, say, Hector Berlioz (a student of twenty when it was first performed), then it would surely have been rejected as eccentric, wilful, and probably incompetent too. And indeed there were many critics and listeners who said just this of the Ninth Symphony, even though it was by Beethoven; the terrible misfortune of deafness, they argued, must have clouded the great man's judgement. But few can really have been happy with this conclusion, apart from the die-hards who cherished eighteenth-century values of taste and moderation, and for whom Beethoven's music had always been too exaggerated, too agitated, too noisy. Romantically-inclined listeners and critics were desperately anxious to find meaning in the final symphonic utterance of the composer universally acknowledged to be the greatest of his age. And the more resistant the work was to interpretation according to the conventions of the day, the more these listeners and critics felt there must be a deeper, more profound meaning to it, if only they could find the key.

In one of his imaginary (or maybe not so imaginary) conversations, Schumann has Karl Voigt, a patron of the arts in Leipzig, say with reference to the Ninth Symphony: 'I am the blind man who is standing before the Strassburg Cathedral, who hears its bells but cannot see the entrance.'[3] Each listener, like Voigt, had to find his or her own way in. Instead of offering ready-made meanings, the Ninth Symphony demanded that the listener participate in the creation of meaning. For instance, the new thematic idea at the end of the first movement (bar 513) clearly sounds like a funeral march. But why is it there, and whose funeral is it? Does it imply that the movement as a whole – or maybe the entire symphony – is a portrait, a biography in music? Or an autobiography? The music asked questions of its listeners; it demanded explanation. And so, in a way that has perhaps never been the case of any other musical work, the Ninth Symphony became a trope, a focus of cultural discourse.

Today we remember the contributions of professional musicians and critics such as Adolph Bernhard Marx and Richard Wagner to this discourse. (As will emerge from this book, the Ninth Symphony we know is Marx's and Wagner's as well as Beethoven's.) But ordinary music lovers took part in it too; there was no professionalized music-analytical jargon to exclude them, as there is nowadays. Of course there was a down side to this. Schumann poked fun at the superficiality, the pretentiousness, the pedantry of much that was said. He pictured a group of Beethovenites arguing about the symphony; some asserted that 'The work seems to contain the different genres of poetry, the first movement being epic, the second, comedy, the third, lyric, the fourth (combining all), the dramatic.' Others 'began to praise the work as being gigantic, colossal, comparable to the Egyptian pyramids. And others painted word pictures: the symphony expresses the story of mankind – first the chaos – then the call of God "There shall be light" – then the sunrise over the first human being, ravished by such splendor – in one word, the whole first chapter of the Pentateuch in this symphony.'[4] In this babble of commentary, a thousand Ninth Symphonies came into existence. And if most of them were pedestrian, a few were imaginative constructions of the first rank.

Of all the works in the mainstream repertory of Western music, the Ninth Symphony seems the most like a construction of mirrors, reflecting and refracting the values, hopes, and fears of those who seek to understand and explain it. One symptom of this is the sheer diversity of interpretations that have been put forward. This has always been the case. A brief notice in the *Allgemeine musikalische Zeitung*, referring to a performance under Mendelssohn in 1841, says that

The grandiose D minor Symphony, the most wonderful, most mysterious, and most subjective work by Beethoven, closed the concert as (in a sense) it closed the artistic life of the great, eternal master. At the same time, it became the keystone of a truly remarkable artistic period, exalted by J. Haydn, Mozart, and Beethoven.[5]

Here the tone is heavily retrospective; the critic treasures the Ninth Symphony because he treasures the past. Nothing could be more different from Wagner's view of the symphony, first promulgated in the previous year; for him, it represented the dawning of a new age in music. From its first performance up to the present day, the Ninth Symphony has inspired diametrically opposed interpretations.

The one thing that all these interpretations have in common is that they treat the Ninth Symphony as a cultural symbol of enormous importance. It had already acquired this symbolic value by the time it became established in the repertory, around the middle of the nineteenth century. Schumann's Beethovenites 'stood there with their eyes popping out, and said: "That was written by our Beethoven, it is a German work – the finale contains a double fugue – he was blamed for not introducing such forms – but how he did it – yes, this is *our* Beethoven"'. And the same sense of possession attaches to the work today, only the focus has changed from the national to the international. The Ninth Symphony has become one of the great symbols of world unity. What other work could possibly have been chosen for a global concert in which choirs and orchestras in Montreal, Moscow, Geneva, and San Francisco performed together, linked by satellite?[6] This is *our* Beethoven and *our* Ninth Symphony – a Ninth Symphony that has been a hundred and seventy years in the making, and that is part of the cultural, intellectual, and political history of those years.

I have incurred many debts in the preparation of this book. A principal one is to Jonathan Del Mar, editor of the Hanover Band Urtext Edition (1988), for contributing the appendix dealing with the complex textual problems that have plagued the symphony ever since its first performance. Qian Yuan supplied me with the Chinese articles discussed in chapter 5, while Jennifer Tong Chee Yee translated them. John Rothgeb supplied me with a pre-publication copy of his translation of the Schenker monograph, and James Webster and Nicholas Marston let me see articles in advance of publication. Irene Suchy let me see her unpublished paper on the Ninth Symphony in Japan. Eric Levi, David Brown, and Jelena Milojkovic-Djuric supplied me with historical information, although it was not always possible to fit it in. To all of these, and to Julian Rushton, my thanks. Finally, the Staatsbibliothek zu Berlin – Preussischer Kulturbesitz, Musikabteilung, kindly permitted me to reproduce p. 111 of Artaria 201 as Ex. 1; Figs. 1 and 2 are reproduced by permission of the Syndics of Cambridge University Library.

1

Sketches and myths

The sketches

One of the best known facts about Beethoven's Ninth Symphony, if it is a fact, is that the work was many years in the making.

We know this because of the sketches. Beethoven sketched as many artists sketch: habitually and perhaps compulsively. He worked things out on paper that other composers of his time worked out in their heads or at the keyboard. Sometimes he doodled; there are sketches that look more like limbering-up exercises or mental diversions than serious attempts at composition. But in other sketches we can see him planning out major works in exhaustive detail, testing and refining them over a period of weeks or months, or even years, before starting to write out the final score. Moreover, Beethoven kept his sketches after the works to which they referred were completed. Every time he moved – which was frequently – the sketches went with him; they were dispersed only after his death.

In his early years, Beethoven sketched on single sheets of paper. Interesting as such sketches may be, there is a limit to what they can tell us, because there is no way of telling in what order they were used. But in 1798, Beethoven started to use sketchbooks rather than single sheets. These sketchbooks were bound before he used them, and on the whole he worked through each book in sequence from the first page to the last. This means that, when a sketchbook has survived intact, we can follow the sketching process more or less as it unfolded. The situation is more complicated when a sketchbook has not survived intact – when it has been divided into separate sections, for instance, or when it has been rebound with the pages in the wrong order. But even then, it is generally possible to work out the original sequence by matching watermarks, the printing of stave lines, the holes made by previous bindings, and the tears on pages that were originally joined together.

The problem with Beethoven's sketches is that he wrote them for his eyes only. One consequence of this is that they are notoriously difficult to read,

Ex. 1 Artaria 201, p. 111

as Ex. 1 demonstrates. But we shouldn't exaggerate this difficulty; reading Beethoven's handwriting is a skill that doctoral students routinely acquire. The real difficulty is one of interpretation. Beethoven generally jotted down no more than a melodic skeleton, perhaps with the addition of a bass line or a few harmony notes, but frequently without clefs, key signatures, or accidentals. We can make sense of so incomplete a representation of the music only by means of an imaginative reconstruction of what he had in mind. But of course this means that what we see in Beethoven's sketches depends on what we expect to see in them. Like a mirror, the sketches for the Ninth Symphony reflect the assumptions of those who interpret them. Hence the myths that surround them.

The origins of the first movement

One of the most striking things about the Ninth Symphony is the opening of the first movement, a rustling *pianissimo* on A and E that builds rapidly up

Table 1 Sketchbooks relevant to the Ninth Symphony

	Desk	Pocket
1815–16	Scheide[a]	
1817–18		Boldrini[b]
1822–3	Artaria 201[c]	
1823	Engelmann[d]	
	Landsberg 8, bundle 1[c]	Artaria 205, bundle 5[c]
1823–4	Landsberg 8, bundle 2[c]	Rolland[d]
		Autograph 8, bundle 1[e]
		Autograph 8, bundle 2[e]

Locations
[a] library of Mr William Scheide, Princeton, New Jersey
[b] lost
[c] Staatsbibliothek zu Berlin – Preussischer Kulturbesitz
[d] Beethovenhaus, Bonn
[e] Biblioteka Jagiellonska, Krakow

to the gigantic theme at bar 17, with its falling D minor arpeggio. This was among Beethoven's earliest ideas for the symphony, and by following its evolution through the sketchbooks we can map out the basic chronology of the compositional process. Table 1 lists the sketchbooks relevant to the Ninth Symphony, and shows the approximate dates when they were in use; it distinguishes between the large format sketchbooks that Beethoven used at home, and the small ones that he could slip into a pocket and use out of doors. The desk sketchbooks naturally tend to contain longer drafts than the pocket ones, and are therefore more important in reconstructing the compositional process.

As it happens, the first trace of the opening of the Ninth Symphony is not in a sketchbook at all; it is on a single sheet of paper in the Liszt archive at Weimar (Ex. 2).[1] Fortunately, this sheet also contains a sketch for a canon called 'Das Schweigen', the final version of which is dated 24 January 1816. So we know that Beethoven had conceived the first few bars of the main theme of the Ninth Symphony, or at any rate of what was to become the main theme of the Ninth Symphony, by early 1816. After that, however, there is no further trace of the theme until the winter of 1817–18, when it turns up in the Boldrini sketchbook. Unfortunately this sketchbook (whose name came from an inscription inside the front cover) went missing at the end of the nineteenth century. This means that we have to rely on the transcriptions from it that

Ex. 2 Sketch of the opening, now in Weimar

were published in the 1870s by Gustav Nottebohm, who was the first scholar to work intensively on Beethoven's sketches, and whose publications laid the foundations for all subsequent sketch studies. Among these publications was an essay on the sketches for the Ninth Symphony, from which Ex. 3 is taken.[2]

While Nottebohm's transcriptions are generally accurate, they are selective. He transcribed what he could read (which often meant what corresponded to the completed composition) and ignored what he couldn't. And he juxtaposed passages regardless of their original position in the sketchbook. But we can still draw some interesting conclusions from his transcription of the Boldrini sketches. The first entry in Ex. 3 has a general resemblance to bars 63–9 of the first movement – the passage leading up to the modulation to B♭ major – while the second is almost identical to bars 469ff; even the instrumentation is shown. Technically speaking, this second entry is simply a major-mode variant of the third and fourth bars of the main theme. But in the context of the coda it becomes one of the most memorable moments of the movement, because of the way in which the D major emerges from D minor, only to fall back into it. It is hard to imagine that Beethoven could have conceived this passage, complete with its instrumentation and with the counter-melody in the second horn, unless he already had some conception of the struggle between D minor and D major that is a feature of the first movement as a whole, and that makes this particular passage so poignant.

The fourth entry in Ex. 3 shows the first four bars of the main theme, much as it appears in the Weimar sheet, together with an abbreviated version of the opening of the symphony as we know it, with its tremolandos on A and E and its descending fourths and fifths in the first violins. There is even something like the D pedal that begins in bar 15 of the finished movement, if Nottebohm's transcription is to be trusted. But the 'u.s.w' ('and so on') at the

Ex. 3 Sketches from the Boldrini sketchbook, transcribed by Nottebohm

end of the transcription is exasperating. Is it Beethoven's 'u.s.w' or Nottebohm's? Does it mean that Beethoven didn't know how to continue the theme, or just that Nottebohm couldn't read what came next? Fortunately there is some additional evidence that we can bring to bear here. In the archives of the publishers Schott, in Mainz, there is a single sheet of paper that dates

Ex. 4 Sketch of the opening, now in Mainz

from around the same time as the Boldrini sketchbook (Ex. 4).[3] Here we see a fuller version of the opening, followed by the first six bars of the main theme in precisely the same form as in the Weimar sheet (including the repetition of bars 3–4 an octave higher), with a new continuation moving towards the dominant. The route to the dominant is still quite unlike that in the final version of the theme. But another single-sheet sketch, dating from a few months later, supplies the missing passage, corresponding to bars 21–4 of the finished movement.[4]

The picture so far is of a remarkably leisurely compositional process, spread over two and a half years, in which the essential elements of the symphony's opening emerged bit by bit. At this point the process came to a complete halt for more than four years – years during which Beethoven was occupied with the late piano sonatas, the Diabelli Variations, and above all the *Missa solemnis*. But in July 1822 Beethoven wrote to his former pupil, Ferdinand Ries, to ask if the Philharmonic Society of London (of which Ries was a member) might be interested in commissioning a 'grand symphony' for its concert series. The directors of the Society decided to offer Beethoven £50 for the work, and Beethoven accepted the commission in December.[5] Work now began in earnest. The final pages of Artaria 201, Beethoven's then current sketchbook, show him mapping out the plan of the symphony as a whole and experimenting in a rather desultory way with the opening of the first movement. And in the first few pages of the next sketchbook, Engelmann, he polished off the last of the Diabelli Variations, thereby clearing the way for intensive work on the Ninth Symphony.

Beethoven started drafting the beginning of the first movement in detail on pp. 13–14 of the Engelmann sketchbook. Ex. 5 is a transcription of the first part of this draft, which dates from around March 1823. The various elements of the sketches from 1816 to 1818 are now incorporated within a fully continuous version of the music. There are still differences between it and the final version, but they are matters of detail rather than of basic conception. We have the sextuplets of the opening, though not the double-stopped bowed *tremolo* of the final version. We have the falling fifths figure, repeated one and then two notches higher and building up into a continuously moving pattern, at first in fifths and subsequently in octaves. All this is essentially the same as in the final version; the principal difference is that in the final version the build-up is tauter and more concentrated, so that the main theme arrives a bar earlier than in the sketch (in bar 17 instead of bar 18).

From here until the end of the main theme there is a bar-for-bar correspondence between the two versions. We find such features as the registral leap in bar 20 (19 in the final version), and the Neapolitan (E♭) harmonization of bar 25 (24). The last four bars of the theme are essentially identical to the final version, too, except that the closing flourish is abbreviated. As for bars 29–32 (28–31 in the final version), Ex. 6 shows how the same melodic pattern underlies both versions; it is just elaborated differently.[6] From a structural point of view, then, as well as in terms of many of its details, the Engelmann sketch shows the opening of the symphony in its final form.

Beethoven's compositional work rarely advanced in the kind of straight line that we might expect, given our knowledge of his compositions in their final form. It's entirely characteristic that a few pages later, on p. 21 of the Engelmann sketchbook, there is a draft in which Beethoven reverted to his

Ex. 5 Sketch of the opening (Englemann sketchbook, pp. 13–14)

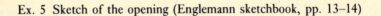

earlier idea of repeating what are bars 19–20 in the final version, as in the Weimar and Mainz sketches; this time he added a portentous pause before the repetition. Nevertheless, the draft in Ex. 5 marks the beginning of the final, sustained compositional process that gave rise to the Ninth Symphony.[7]

Ex. 6

Ex. 7 Scheide sketchbook, p. 51

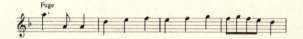

Although Beethoven now and then jotted down ideas for one movement while working on another, he basically worked on each movement in turn. The first movement was probably finished in the early summer of 1823, the second in late summer, the third in the autumn, and the finale in February 1824.

The origins of the second and third movements

All this provides good grounds for saying that the opening of the Ninth Symphony, and indeed the first movement as a whole, was many years in the making. But the situation is more complicated when it comes to the other movements. Each of them embodies materials that can be traced back before 1823. What is not clear is at what stage Beethoven began to think of these materials in the context of the Ninth Symphony, or indeed of a symphony at all.

Histories of the Ninth Symphony usually begin with an isolated entry that Beethoven made in the winter of 1815–16, on p. 51 of the Scheide sketchbook (Ex. 7). As Sir George Grove put it in his influential book on Beethoven's symphonies, this represents 'the germ of the Scherzo of the Ninth Symphony'.[8] Or at least that is what it represents to us. What it represented to

9

Ex. 8 Fugued opening from the Weimar sheet (see Ex. 2)

Beethoven when he wrote it is harder to say. There is some reason to think that he intended it for a symphony, because at the bottom of the same page there is a memorandum that reads 'Symphony at the beginning only 4 voices 2 Vi[oli]n, Viol[a], Bass amongst them forte with other voices and if possible bring in all the other instruments one by one'. And the Weimar sheet containing the first sketch for the opening of the Ninth Symphony, which was probably written soon afterwards, also includes a fugued tune that resembles the Scherzo of the Ninth Symphony, though less closely (Ex. 8).[9] The tunes in Exx. 7 and 8 were, or became, closely associated in Beethoven's mind; both can be found in sketches for the Scherzo, up to quite a late stage in the compositional process.

All this might suggest that the basic idea for the Scherzo of the Ninth Symphony goes back at least as far as that for the first movement, and that the two were from the beginning associated with one another. But there is a complication. In 1817, Beethoven began a movement for string quintet which is known to modern scholars as Hess 40.[10] It starts with a slow introduction, followed by the first four bars of a fugue based on the subject from Ex. 8; at this point it breaks off. Does this mean that Ex. 8 was intended for a string quintet rather for a symphony? (The layout of Ex. 8 suggests so.) And in that case is it just coincidence that Beethoven sketched it on the same sheet as what

Ex. 9 Beethovenhaus, BSk 20, fol. 1ʳ

became the opening of the Ninth Symphony? Or did he have two uses in mind for the tune? It is impossible to answer these questions, and therefore impossible to know when Beethoven first conceived the Scherzo of the Ninth Symphony.

The situation is still more confused in the case of the slow movement. As a double variation set, it has two themes, each of which was conceived in the context of something other than the slow movement of the Ninth Symphony. The Andante moderato theme first appears around April 1823, but in the context of a minuet and trio; only later did Beethoven think of using it in the slow movement.[11] As for the Adagio molto theme, it is hard to say when this first appeared, because it emerged by degrees. Exx. 9–11 pick out some of the stages in this process.

Ex. 9, which dates from autumn 1822, seems to have been intended for the first movement of a symphony other than the Ninth, with a slow introduction in E♭ major followed by an Allegro in C minor.[12] The slow introduction recurs, in the same key, on the final page of Artaria 201, where it follows the sketches that Beethoven made for the Ninth Symphony in the winter of 1822–23. It next appears, in a rhythmic variant, on p. 24 of the Engelmann sketchbook; this time it has been transposed to B♭ major, and is marked '2nd movement'. Then it turns up, again in B♭ major, on p. 38 of Landsberg 8, Bundle 2, which dates from around April 1823 (Ex. 10);[13] it is now marked as being for the third movement, and is linked to another variant of the Scherzo idea, apparently as an alternative to the Allegro theme of Ex. 9. Finally Ex. 11 shows an easily recognizable version of the Adagio theme from the Ninth Symphony dating from around July 1823, which retains the same opening as Exx. 9 and 10;[14] Beethoven vacillated for a long time between this opening and the one we know.

It seems obvious enough that Ex. 9 is not a sketch for the slow movement

Ex. 10 Landsberg 8, Bundle 2, p. 38

Ex. 11 Landsberg 8, Bundle 2, p. 77

of the Ninth Symphony, and that Ex. 11 is. But it is not at all obvious just where the transition occurs. Ex. 10 is particularly unsettling; it confuses what we would like to think of both as separate movements and as separate symphonies. It suggests that, even as he was completing the first movement of the Ninth Symphony, Beethoven was far from decided as to what form the remaining movements would take, or indeed how many symphonies he was composing.

A tale of two symphonies

Even in 1818, before the four-year break in the compositional process, there seems to have been some question as to how many symphonies Beethoven was writing. At least that is the impression given by the famous memorandum describing an 'Adagio cantique', which was written on the back of a sketch for the *Hammerklavier* Sonata, and for that reason can be assigned to around April or May 1818.[15] As translated by Alexander Wheelock Thayer, the first great biographer of Beethoven, the memorandum runs as follows:

Adagio cantique

Pious song in a symphony in ancient modes – Lord God we praise Thee – alleluia – either alone or as introduction to a fugue. The whole 2nd sinfonie might be characterized in this manner in which case the vocal parts would enter in the last movement or already in the Adagio. The violins, etc., of the orchestra to be increased tenfold in the last movement, in which case the vocal parts would enter gradually – in the text of the Adagio Greek myth, *Cantique Ecclesiastique* – in the Allegro, feast of Bachus [*sic*].[16]

The memorandum could hardly be more suggestive in its mention of vocal parts in the last movement, to say nothing of the ancient modes and the indication of a massive orchestration. And the idea of the vocal parts entering gradually is reminiscent of the instruments entering one by one in the Scheide memorandum of 1815–16. Clearly these ideas fed into the Ninth Symphony. But in that case what are we to make of the reference to a '2nd sinfonie'? Thayer, who based his account of the sketches on Nottebohm's, concluded from this reference that Beethoven was thinking of the symphony in ancient modes as a separate project from the one whose opening he had already sketched.

After the four-year break, in 1822, Beethoven still seems to have been thinking of two symphonies. That, at any rate, is what Nottebohm concluded from the first sketch that Beethoven made after resuming work on the Ninth Symphony, on p. 111 of Artaria 201 (Ex. 1). Nottebohm's transcription of the relevant passage, which is on the bottom five lines of the page, is shown in Ex. 12. In translation, the text reads: 'The symphony in 4 movements, with the second in 2/4 . . . could be in 6/8, and the 4th movement'[17] – and then comes the opening of the Scherzo, in its Weimar version, together with the indication 'well fugued'. Of the finale, as we know it, there is no trace. And thereby hangs a tale.

Ex. 12 Nottebohm's transcription of Artaria 201, p. 11 (see Ex. 1)

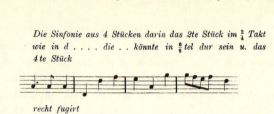

Die Sinfonie aus 4 Stücken darin das 2te Stück im $\frac{2}{4}$ Takt wie in d . . . . die . . könnte in $\frac{6}{8}$ tel dur sein u. das 4te Stück

recht fugirt

As Nottebohm read page 111 of Artaria 201, the implication is that, at this stage, the symphony was to have concluded with an instrumental finale. And Nottebohm linked this with a memorandum that Beethoven entered just a few pages later, on page 119. In Thayer's translation, it runs as follows:

Sinfonie allemand after which the chorus

Freude – de schö – ner Göt – ter – fun – ken Toch – ter aus E – ly – si – um

enters or also without variations. End of the Sinfonie with Turkish music and vocal chorus.

A 'German' symphony: that, argued Nottebohm, must mean as opposed to the one for the Philharmonic Society. In other words, he reasoned, as in 1818, Beethoven was planning *two* symphonies: one, for London, with an instrumental finale, and the other (the German one) with a finale based on Schiller's 'An die Freude' – though using a different tune from the one we know. And Nottebohm found further confirmation of his theory in a letter written by the musical journalist and novelist, Friedrich Rochlitz, describing a meeting with Beethoven in 1822. In this letter, Rochlitz claimed to be quoting Beethoven verbatim:

For some time I have been occupied with three other major works. Much of the music has already hatched, at least in my head. I must first get them off my neck: two important symphonies, each one different from my others, and an oratorio. It will take a long time, you see, since for some time now I have not been able to bring myself to work easily. I sit and think and think; I have had it for a long time, but I can't get it down on paper. These big works are always hard to get started. Once I'm into them, they go well.[18]

In this way the story of the two symphonies entered the literature. Thayer accepted Nottebohm's argument:

The conclusions to be drawn from the sketches thus far are that, as was the case in 1812 when the Seventh and Eighth Symphonies were brought forth as a pair, Beethoven was again contemplating the almost simultaneous production of two symphonies. . . . It may be assumed . . . that the present Symphony in D minor was associated in Beethoven's mind with the English commission, and that the second . . . was to have been a 'Sinfonie allemand'. For a time, at least, Beethoven is not likely to have contemplated a choral movement with German words in connection with the symphony for the London Philharmonic Society: this was to have an instrumental finale. The linguistic objection would be invalid in the case of the German symphony, however, and to this was now assigned the contemplated setting of Schiller's poem.

And so Thayer traced the subsequent history of the Ninth Symphony as a merging of these two, originally distinct, plans. Virtually every subsequent writer on the subject has based his account on Thayer and told the same story. It has become received knowledge.

The story is based on three pieces of evidence. First, there is Rochlitz's letter, which is addressed to the publisher G. C. Härtel and dated 1822; the original does not survive, but the text was published in 1827. In this letter, Rochlitz says that the meeting at which Beethoven told him about the two symphonies took place in Baden. Now Beethoven usually went to Baden in the summer. But it so happens that Beethoven was in Döbling at the time when Rochlitz says he met him. There is no good reason to believe that the two met at all. Indeed there's no good reason to believe that the letter ever existed as such; Rochlitz probably wrote the text for publication in 1827, putting Härtel's name on it because Härtel had died the previous year and so could not expose the forgery.[19] Rochlitz had a talent for invention; it seems clear that he was the author of the famous letter (first published in the journal Rochlitz edited, the *Allgemeine musikalische Zeitung*) in which Mozart described how his works appeared to him 'like a beautiful statue'. Rochlitz had the knack of improving on reality; he said what Mozart and Beethoven *ought* to have said, at least in the eyes of nineteenth-century romantics. And so his fabrications were widely believed.

The second piece of evidence is Beethoven's memorandum about the 'Sinfonie allemand'. Nottebohm's theory that this implies the existence of some other symphony ties in with the evidence that Beethoven had roughed out a new symphonic opening a few months earlier (that is, Ex. 9). But two qualifications have to be made. First, there is no particular reason to think that the symphony beginning as in Ex. 9 was to have a choral conclusion, or even that Beethoven had got as far as considering what sort of conclusion it might have. Second, the memorandum about the 'Sinfonie allemand' was written at a time when Beethoven was clearly running through all sorts of possible projects in his mind. On the very same page, there is another memorandum which reads 'also, instead of a new symphony, a new overture on [the name] Bach, very fugato with three trombones';[20] on the opposite page, there is a memorandum about a quintet in C minor. There is an obvious danger of inflating what may have been no more than passing thoughts into long-term strategies on Beethoven's part.

The final and most important piece of evidence for the story of the two symphonies is page 111 of Artaria 201, with its indication of an instrumental finale. It's worth trying to match Nottebohm's transcription with the bottom five lines of the facsimile in Ex. 1. The transcription begins half way through the fourth line from the bottom, with 'Die Sinfonie aus 4 Stücken'. Beethoven's text runs continuously from there until 'u. das 4te Stück', at the bottom of the page. And then he writes 'Vi=100'. This is an example of the elaborate system of cross-references that Beethoven used when he ran out of space and had to continue what he was writing somewhere else. The 'Vi' is the first half of the Latin word 'Vide', or 'see'; he would write the 'de' at the point where the entry continued, together with the identifying number. In this case you can see the '=de 100' at the beginning of the fifth line from the bottom. And it is followed by the scherzo theme, just as Nottebohm transcribed it.

But close inspection shows that Nottebohm's reading is wrong.[21] For one thing, the '=de 100' is written *over* the scherzo theme. For another, the spacing and the appearance of the writing indicates that Beethoven wrote 'recht fugirt' (which, of course, refers to the scherzo theme) *before* he wrote 'Die Sinfonie aus 4 Stücken . . .'. And what all this means is that the '=de 100' does not go with the scherzo theme at all. It goes with the seventh line from the bottom – which shows the first four bars of the 'Ode to Joy' theme exactly as we know it, complete with Schiller's words.

When he resumed work on the Ninth Symphony in the winter of 1822–3, then, Beethoven already had in mind a finale based on the 'Ode to Joy'. The story of the two symphonies, one with a vocal and the other with an instrumental finale, has no real foundation in the sources. But it arose through something more than a simple mistake. It represented something that later critics of Beethoven's music were predisposed to believe. For them, the greatest challenge of the symphony was its vocal finale, blending the symphonic genre with Schiller's words. Critics influenced by Wagner saw the finale as marking the end of the purely instrumental symphony and the beginning of the music drama; others saw it as an appalling lapse of taste. But they all saw it as representing a kind of cross-roads in the evolution of the genre. And it was precisely this conception that the story of the two symphonies dramatized.

Nottebohm's essay on the sketches for the Ninth Symphony was first published in 1876, the same year as Brahms's First Symphony. The finale of Brahms's symphony contains something suspiciously near to a quotation of Beethoven's 'Joy' theme. This quotation, or misquotation, was widely interpreted by listeners and commentators as implying a correction of the wrong turn that Beethoven had made fifty years earlier. It was this climate of opinion that gave Nottebohm's account of the two symphonies its credibility: the story was believed not because there was good evidence for it, but because it struck a chord with the concerns of the later nineteenth century. It was, in other words, a myth.

Doubts over the finale

The myth didn't stop here. Readers of Thayer, or of any of the writers based on Thayer (and that means everybody), will know that Beethoven had serious doubts about the choral finale even as he was composing it, and actually wrote down the main melody for an alternative, instrumental version of the movement. As usual, the source for this is Nottebohm. In his essay on the Ninth Symphony, Nottebohm gives a sequence of transcriptions from the sketches to bolster this argument. He begins with a verbal remark, 'perhaps however the chorus Joy sweet gods' (the implication being, as opposed to an instrumental finale).[22] Then come three musical transcriptions, each representing a slightly different version of what eventually became the main theme of the finale of the A minor quartet, Op. 132. And the first of these, which is shown in Ex. 13, bears the inscription 'Finale instromentale'. Nottebohm's message is clear enough even without his accompanying text; the idea of Beethoven's vacillating over the choral finale seems to have been irresistible to him, for the reasons I have just explained.

But the evidence is by no means as hard as Nottebohm suggests. The remark about the chorus, to be sure, comes shortly before Beethoven began intensive work on the finale – just where, if anywhere, one would expect to find him him vacillating. (Even so, it would make more sense if it *followed* a series of sketches for an instrumental finale; otherwise what does the 'however' refer

Ex. 13 Autograph 8, Bundle 2, fol. 8ʳ

to?) Nottebohm's first and second music examples, however, date from the last stages of the composition of the finale. And his final example comes two pages *after* the last sketches for the finale; as Robert Winter puts it, this sketch 'no longer has anything to do with the history of the Ninth'.[23]

There is, however, another entry that predates any of these and that clearly *does* have to do with the history of the Ninth; it shows what looks very much like an early version of the 'finale instromentale' tune, beginning with the same tremolando harmonies (Ex. 14).[24] Moreover, it is headed 'Finale' and bears the annotation 'vor der Freude' ('before the Joy [theme]'). It is, in short, one of the many outline sketches Beethoven made for the instrumental introduction to the finale. And this suggests a simpler explanation for the whole sequence of entries than Nottebohm's: Beethoven rejected this idea for the introduction to the finale, but went on sketching it sporadically with a view to using it for something other than the Ninth Symphony (maybe he had already started thinking about the late quartets). Seen this way, the evidence of serious vacillation ceases to be very substantial at all.[25]

Nottebohm saw the sketch in Ex. 14. In fact he reproduced it on page 187 of his essay, along with other sketches for the introduction to the finale. But he did not connect it with the later one marked 'finale instromentale'. The later sketch in fact comes seven pages *earlier* in his essay, making it hard for Nottebohm's readers to reconstruct the actual sequence of events. In effect, his presentation prejudges the issue. I don't mean to say that Nottebohm was deliberately twisting the evidence for his own ends. On the contrary, he was a dedicated scholar whose success in bringing order to the apparent chaos of Beethoven's sketches astonished his contemporaries. Indeed his very authority inhibited subsequent Beethoven scholars; for nearly a century they relied on his transcriptions of the sketches, rather than going back to the sources for themselves.

In relying on Nottebohm in this way, these scholars did him a disservice. They treated the transcription of Beethoven's sketches as if it were a purely

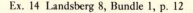

Ex. 14 Landsberg 8, Bundle 1, p. 12

mechanical process, as distinct from making sense of them. But that was a basic error. As I said, Beethoven's sketches have to be interpreted rather than simply read. And the manner in which Nottebohm interpreted what he saw, and presented the results of his work, inevitably reflected his own concerns and values, and those of the time at which he lived. His writings embody a nineteenth-century view of Beethoven's music.

The first performance

Although the Philharmonic Society commissioned the Ninth Symphony, the first performance was not given in London; indeed it seems as if the Society did not receive a copy of the score until the end of 1824, six months after the Vienna premiere.[26] Beethoven had reservations about giving the first performance in Vienna, but these were not occasioned by any sense of obligation to the Philharmonic Society; they were the result of his disaffection with Viennese musical life. In the 1820s, symphonic music had become a minority taste. What attracted popular and fashionable interest in Vienna was the Italian opera, and this was intensified by the three-month visit of an Italian opera company under Domenico Barbaja in 1822; Rossini himself attended the performances. According to Beethoven's admittedly unreliable amanuensis, Anton Schindler, the audience's enthusiasm 'grew from performance to performance until it degenerated into a general intoxication of the senses whose sole inspiration was the virtuosity of the singers'. By 1823, he says, 'What was left of appreciation of German vocal music disappeared entirely. From this year dates the deplorable state of all music.'[27]

The February petition

Under these circumstances, Beethoven began to explore the possibility of giving the first performance of the Ninth Symphony in Berlin. Hearing of this,

19

a group of his patrons and supporters published a letter in which they asked him to think again. 'Although the name and creations of Beethoven belong to all the world and to those lands where art finds a welcoming spirit,' they wrote,

yet it is Austria that may claim him as its own. There still lives in its people the appreciation of the great and immortal works that Mozart and Haydn created within its bosom for all time, and with happy pride they know that the sacred triad, in which their names and yours shine as symbols of the highest in the spiritual realm of tones, sprang from the earth of the Fatherland. . . . We know that a new flower glows in the garland of your noble and still unequalled symphonies. . . . Need we tell you that as all glances turned hopefully to you, all perceived with sorrow that the one man we are compelled to name as the foremost of all living men in his field looked on in silence as foreign art invaded German soil, the place of honour of the German muse?[28]

The signatories of this extraordinary document, which dates from February 1824, were not just appealing to Beethoven as the champion of German art in the face of the Italian onslaught. They were appealing to him as the sole remaining representative of a musical tradition that they saw as in danger of disappearing; there is something strangely retrospective about the mention of the 'holy triad' consisting of Beethoven and his two illustrious, but long dead, forebears. In this way, Beethoven's Ninth Symphony was from the very first associated with what in the 1830s and 40s would become a full-blown revivalist movement, the result of which was the establishment of the classical repertory as we know it today – a more or less fixed and unchanging repertory of 'great and immortal works', as the petition put it, against which any contemporary productions are inevitably measured. I shall return to this.

The petition had the desired effect. Arrangements were set in motion for a Viennese premiere, at which the overture *Die Weihe des Hauses* and the Kyrie, Credo, and Agnus Dei from the *Missa solemnis* were also to be given for the first time; the *Akademie* (as such concerts were called) was eventually fixed for May 7 in the Kärntnerthor Theater. It's generally said, because Thayer says it, that there were only two rehearsals for this premiere. This is true, but misleading. There were two *full* rehearsals, but there were also sectional rehearsals for the strings, as well as separate rehearsals for the chorus. As for the soloists, they were coached by Beethoven himself, with Michael Umlauf assisting. (At least that is what Thayer says. In practice it is likely to have been the other way round, because of Beethoven's deafness.) Schindler recounts how the soloists pleaded with Beethoven to eliminate some of the highest notes from their parts; Beethoven refused in virtually every case, telling the singers that they had been spoiled by performing too much Italian music. He rejected similar requests from the chorus-master, even though Umlauf gave them his support. 'No one could remember that he had ever been so obdurate in the past', writes Schindler.[29] And he adds darkly: 'When a composer, contrary to his own best interests and judgement, treats the human voice like an instrument, the only thing he can do is wage a peevish war in defence of his caprice.'

While all this was going on, speculation about the event was mounting in the press. It had been fuelled by the February petition, which had been published in the *Wiener allgemeine musikalische Zeitung* and *Wiener Theater-Zeitung*. (The publication had created rumours that Beethoven was himself the author of the petition, further infuriating the composer.[30]) On 1 May, a week before the concert, the *Theater-Zeitung* published a notice that surpassed even the petition in its nationalist tones:

This Academie will occasion celebration among friends of German music and offer recognition of the national master. Certainly France and England will envy us the opportunity of making personal homage to Beethoven, who is acknowledged to be the supreme composer in the entire world. Anybody who cares for the great and the beautiful will be present this evening.

7 May, 1824

The concert finally took place, as scheduled, at 7 pm on 7 May. Published accounts of the event agree that the hall was packed, with the exception of the imperial box; a dissonant note is sounded only by a certain Joseph Carl Rosenbaum, who noted in his diary that many of the boxes were empty.[31] The regular orchestra and chorus of the Kärntnerthor Theater (who were more used to performing Rossini than Beethoven) had been supplemented for the occasion by amateurs belonging to the Gesellschaft der Musikfreunde; as a result, there were twenty-four violins, ten violas, twelve cellos and basses, and double the usual number of winds.[32] The review of the concert in the most influential music journal of the time, the *Allgemeine musikalische Zeitung*, makes it less than clear exactly who was in control of this ensemble; according to it, 'Hr. Schuppanzigh directed at the violin, Hr. Kapellmeister Umlauf directed with the baton, and the composer himself took part in the general direction of everything.'[33] But it is evident that it was really Umlauf who was in charge. Friedrich Kanne, who reviewed the concert in the *Wiener allgemeine musikalische Zeitung*, spoke of his 'truly outstanding skill. . . . His eye, with lightning speed, met every solo's entrance, and inspired every member to energetic effort.'[34]

Beethoven stood at Umlauf's side, with the score on a stand in front of him. Over seventy years later, an eye-witness – by then in her nineties – told Felix Weingartner, the conductor, that although Beethoven had seemed to be following the music, he turned over several pages at once at the end of each movement.[35] His role was supposedly to indicate the tempo at the beginning of each movement. But he evidently did more than this. Kanne speaks of 'the transfigured master . . . following the score, experiencing and at the same time indicating each little nuance and rise of the performance'. The violinist, Joseph Böhm, chose his words less kindly:

Beethoven himself conducted, that is, he stood in front of a conductor's stand and threw himself back and forth like a madman. At one moment he stretched to his full height, at the next he crouched down to the floor, he flailed about with his hands and feet as though he wanted to play all the instruments and sing all the chorus parts. – The actual direction was in Duport's[36] hands; we musicians followed his baton only.[37]

Indeed Sigismund Thalberg, the virtuoso pianist and composer, who was in the audience, told Thayer that 'Umlauf told the choir and orchestra to pay no attention whatever to Beethoven's beating of the time but all to watch him.'[38]

It is easier to reconstruct how the concert looked than how it sounded. The *Theater-Zeitung* critic was sympathetic:

With regard to the orchestra one can say no more than that it is inconceivable how they were able to perform these uncommonly difficult compositions with three [*sic*] rehearsals, because they performed them admirably. And this orchestra was composed for the most part of dilettantes; that one can only find in Vienna! [This remark, of course, cuts both ways.] The singers did what they could. . . . The intonation makes this composition very difficult to sing, and besides that the rhythm changes very frequently.

The correspondent for the *Allgemeine musikalische Zeitung* was a shade more explicit. He described it as

a performance that could in no way suffice in view of the extraordinary difficulties, especially in the vocal sections. . . . The necessary differentiation of light and dark, security of intonation, fine shading, and nuanced execution were all lacking.

But others were more direct. In his review, Kanne said of the Scherzo that

A composition such as this, characterized by the utmost freedom of spirit and unbridled creativity, often scarcely gives time for trained violinists to think out a good fingering.

. . . Weak players . . . set down their bows and sat out so many measures. . . . The reliable ones, with true artistic ability, had to play more loudly during such passages, compensating for the players who swallowed their notes.

There were problems in the finale, too. Leopold Sonnleithner, who was in the audience, recalled forty years later that 'The double-bass players had not the faintest idea what they were supposed to do with the recitatives. One heard nothing but a gruff rumbling in the basses, almost as though the composer had intended to offer practical evidence that instrumental music is absolutely incapable of speech.'[39] As for the chorus, Schindler says that 'when they could not reach the high notes as written, the sopranos simply did not sing'.[40]

Whether because of the quality of performance or for other reasons, Joseph Carl Rosenbaum was unimpressed. 'For all the large forces', he wrote in his diary, 'little effect. B's disciples clamoured, most of the audience stayed quiet, many did not wait for the end.' One gets the impression that Herr Rosenbaum did not greatly care for modern music. Certainly the *Allgemeine musikalische Zeitung* critic thought differently. After listing the shortcomings of the performance, he continues:

And yet the effect was indescribably great and magnificent; everybody offered jubilant and heart-felt applause to the master, whose inexhaustible genius had shown us a new world, revealing the magical secrets of a holy art that we had never before heard or imagined!

And the *Theater-Zeitung* concurred:

The public received the musical hero with the utmost respect and sympathy, listened to his wonderful, gigantic creations with the most absorbed attention and broke out in jubilant applause, often during sections, and repeatedly at the end of them.

One of the sections that was interrupted in this way was the Scherzo; several reports mention that spontaneous applause broke out at the entry of the timpani. Some accounts say it was at the end of this movement that Beethoven stood, leafing through the pages of his score, until Caroline Unger, the contralto soloist, tapped him on the shoulder and turned him so that he could see the audience applauding wildly; others say it happened at the end of the concert.

Caroline Unger tapping the deaf composer's shoulder (or, in other accounts, plucking him by the sleeve) as he stood there leafing his pages (or, in other accounts, still beating time, unaware that the music had stopped): this is one of the dominant images in the myth-making process that began as memories of the concert faded. Half a century later, Elliott Graeme (who was *not* there) recreated the occasion. The music, he says, seemed to act upon the immense mass of human beings that thronged the building in every part, like ambrosial nectar; they became intoxicated with delight, and when the refrain was caught up by the choir, *'Seid umschlungen, Millionen!'* a shout of exuberant joy rent the air, completely drowning the singers and instruments. But there stood the master in the midst, his face turned towards the orchestra, absorbed and sunk within himself as usual, – he heard nothing, saw nothing. Fräulein Unger, the soprano, turned him gently round, and then what a sight met his astonished gaze, – a multitude transported with joy! Almost all were standing, and the greater number melted to tears, now for the first time realizing fully the extent of Beethoven's calamity. Probably in all that great assembly the master himself was the most unmoved. Simply bowing in response to the ovation, he left the theatre gloomy and despondent, and took his homeward way in silence.[41]

This splendidly romanticized account inserts its interpretation into the gaps between the recorded facts. But it goes beyond that. It recasts the facts in its own image. Quite apart from turning Caroline Unger into a soprano, it transfers the whole incident to the most spiritually intense moment of the symphony. Graeme's finest touch, however, is the picture of a dour and taciturn Beethoven stumping off home. Here we have quite explicit evidence concerning the real sequence of events – evidence of which Graeme must have known. In his biography, Schindler tells what happened after the concert.

The government official Joseph Hüttenbrenner, who still lives in Vienna, helped me bring home the exhausted master. I then handed Beethoven the box–office report. When he saw it, he collapsed. We picked him up and laid him on the sofa. We stayed at his side until late that night; he refused both food and drink, then said no more. Finally, when we noticed that Morpheus had gently closed his eyes, we withdrew. The next morning his servants found him sleeping as we had left him, still dressed in the suit he had worn in the concert-hall.[42]

This incident itself provides further grist to the myth-making mill. Romain Rolland, whose little book *Beethoven* became the bible of the Beethoven cult that grew up in France before the First World War, tells the story as follows:

The Symphony raised frantic enthusiasm. Many wept. Beethoven fainted with emotion after the concert; he was taken to Schindler's house, where he remained asleep all the night and the following morning, fully dressed, neither eating nor drinking. The triumph was only fleeting, however, and the concert brought in nothing for Beethoven. His material circumstances of life were not changed by it. He found himself poor, ill, alone but a conqueror: conqueror of the mediocrity of mankind, conqueror of his destiny, conqueror of his suffering. 'Sacrifice, always sacrifice the trifles of life to art! God is over all!'[43]

Nothing could more tellingly illustrate the myth-making process than the contrast between Rolland's Beethoven, who faints with emotion as the audience cheers wildly, and Schindler's Beethoven – surely on this occasion the real Beethoven – who collapses when he sees how little money the concert has brought in.

2

Early impressions

Vienna, 1824

I have quoted enough extracts from the reviews that followed the premiere, and a repeat performance given a fortnight later, for their general tone to be clear: despite the shortcomings in the orchestra and chorus, the critics agreed, the great Beethoven had again proved himself to be at the height of his creative powers. But how did these earliest critics of the Ninth Symphony actually hear the music? How did they respond to its sonorities, themes, and forms? Some of them seem to have been too overcome to enter into details: 'After a single hearing of these immense compositions', wrote the *Theater-Zeitung* correspondent, 'one can scarcely say more than that one has heard them. To engage in an illuminating discussion is impossible for anyone who only attended the performance.' But other critics were prepared to attempt the impossible, writing unusually long and detailed reports on the music. Of these, Kanne was probably the only one who had seen the score; he visited Beethoven in late May to look at it.[1]

In what follows, I shall try to set these critics' responses into the context of the musical form as it might be seen today.

First movement

The correspondent for the *Allgemeine musikalische Zeitung* described the opening movement as

a defiantly bold Allegro in D minor, most ingenious in its invention and worked out with true athletic power. There is continuous suspense from the first chord (A major) up to the colossal theme that gradually emerges from it; but it is resolved in a satisfying manner.

It is striking that this critic describes the opening chord as A major, when Beethoven so pointedly omits the third; one has the impression that the basic

26

idea of the opening, with the sound as it were welling up from nowhere, was lost on him. Nevertheless, his emphasis on the music's large spans of tension and relaxation captures one of its characteristic qualities, as does his description of the first theme as 'colossal'. By contrast, the critic from the *Theater-Zeitung* (who attempted a more detailed discussion after the repeat performance) resorted to poetic metaphor so as to convey his impressions of the movement: 'All the joys and sufferings of the human soul resound here in the most varied forms', he wrote; they 'intertwine in marvellous, magic knots that unravel and again weave themselves into new and wonderful signs.' In pointing to the broad range of emotions encompassed within the movement – to its universality – this critic anticipates the tone of much subsequent commentary.

But it is Kanne who gives us the most vivid impression of how the music struck him:

Like a volcano, Beethoven's power of imagination tears the earth asunder when it tries to check his fiery progress; with marvellous persistence, it develops figures which at first sight seem almost bizarre but which the master, through his skill, transforms into a stream of graceful elaborations that refuse to end, swinging upward, step by step, to ever more brilliant heights. With inexhaustible creative power, the master places new obstacles in the path of his upward-rushing stream of fire. He impedes it with tied figures that cut across one other. . . . He inverts his phrases, forcing them down into terrifying depths, and then uniting them in a ray that stands out against the clouds and disappears high up in an entirely unexpected unison. . . . He gives the eye no rest! . . . [He] transforms the entire mass of his figures into a transfigured, blue fire, like a scene painter.

Kanne dramatizes the quality of antagonism that subsequent commentators developed into fully-fledged scenarios: the earth tries to impede the rage of Beethoven's fire, tied figures (presumably those of bars 80ff, 132ff, 218ff, and 477ff) place new obstacles in its path, phrases are forced down into the depths. And in suggesting that the struggle is Beethoven's struggle, Kanne opens the door to the autobiographical interpretations of the symphony that dominated Beethoven criticism in the later part of the nineteenth century. But above all, Kanne constructs a poetic analogue to the constant flux of Beethoven's music. He attempts to recreate the music's effect in words – rather than trying to explain it in musical terms, as a modern critic would.

Nowadays we might describe the basic plan of this movement as a fairly straightforward example of sonata form. It is easy enough to locate its main structural points, using what since the middle of the last century has been the conventional analytical terminology for such forms. The exposition runs to bar 160, and is followed by what at first seems to be a repeat of the entire section. But after a few bars the music turns in a new direction: this is not the traditional repeat of the exposition, but the development section. The recapitulation begins with the prolonged *fortissimo* of bar 301, and finally, at bar 427, there is a coda one hundred and twenty bars long.

What is not so conventional is the manner in which the plan is carried through. Most striking is the sheer multiplicity of subsidiary materials. Any attempt to categorize them individually, as is usual when analyzing music in sonata form, leads to an uncontrolled proliferation of labels; Beethoven conceals the sonata plan behind a mass of thematic detail that is constantly renewed from moment to moment. And the repeated avoidance of strong cadences, together with a consistent tendency for harmonic resolutions to occur on weak beats, adds to the effect of continual motion.[2] Hence the impression, as Kanne described it, of a stream of graceful elaborations that refuse to end, giving the eye no rest.

But we can pick out the main elements in this stream of elaborations. The open fifths of the opening emerge out of silence, steadily building up to the first main subject in D minor, at bar 17, with its craggy contours of melody and rhythm. (It is hard to describe the Ninth Symphony without resorting to images of mountains.) The whole process is now repeated, but leading to B♭ major instead of D minor (bar 51); in this way Beethoven introduces and links the two principal keys around which the movement is constructed. The music turns back to D minor at bar 57, before settling finally in B♭ major for the second main subject; the augmented fourth in the bass at bar 72 (C–G♭) is decisive in establishing the new key.

In conventional analytical terms it would be a mistake to call the lyrical melodic figure of bar 74 the second subject; it is just an introductory figure, leading to the second subject proper at bar 80. But this is an example of the divergence between analysis and the listener's experience of the music. The figure at bar 74 is clear and memorable, whereas the melody of bar 80 seems curiously indistinct – not least because of its orchestration, with the melody being split between the different woodwind instruments, and the bass line obscuring both rhythmic and harmonic structure. Moreover, the figure at bar 74 clearly prefigures the 'Joy' theme of the finale; at least, people have heard it this way for more than a century. (More on this in chapter 5.) As a result of all this, the figure at bar 74 has an importance that conventional analysis would deny it.

The music proceeds in a series of great waves from here to the end of the exposition (images of the sea, too, constantly recur in descriptions of this movement). The first wave includes not only the second subject proper, but the distinct subsidiary figures at bars 88 and 92, reaching a climax with the dotted-note figure at bar 102. Now there is a sudden collapse, in terms of tonality as well as dynamics: the B major of bar 108 creates the effect of a tonal daydream, so to speak, dissipating the momentum that had earlier been built up towards closure in B♭. This collapse begins the second great wave, which grows in intensity through the subsidiary figures at bars 120 and 132. Its momentum is again checked at bar 138, where the strangely intricate woodwind writing demands a slight relaxation of tempo; older commentators sometimes called this the third subject. But it outlines a straightforward cadential progression, and from this point on the music moves rapidly and directly towards the end of the exposition, which is marked at bar 150 by dotted-note arpeggio figures drawn from the first subject.

As I said, the development section begins as if it were a repeat of the exposition. But the first main theme, in D minor, never arrives. Instead the music remains *pianissimo*, moving through D major and G minor, until the rapid *crescendo* at bar 186; this leads to an emphatic cadence in G minor using the dotted-note arpeggio figure from the end of the exposition. There now begins a long passage based on figures drawn from the first subject (compare bars 17 and 19 with bars 198 and 192 respectively). At first the music is almost exaggeratedly relaxed, with its easy-going sequences (bars 192 and 194) and ritardandos (bars 195 and 213). But at bar 218 it stiffens. There is a mock fugato, based on the figure from bar 19 but exploiting the tied notes to which Kanne referred; this begins in C minor, but moves through a number of tonal regions before settling down in A minor from around bar 250, with another series of relaxed sequences. What is perhaps most striking about the whole section from bar 192 to bar 274, particularly in the context of what came before, is the way in which the music *doesn't* build up towards a climax. Beethoven gives us a genial flow of music at the point when we might most expect tension and drama. He seems to be writing not with the musical form, but against it.

The final phase of the development begins with the second subject material at bar 275. From here there is a single tonal trajectory from A minor through F major to the beginning of recapitulation; the material from bar 19 returns at bar 287, where the high string writing sounds more like Bruckner or Mahler than Beethoven. And then at bar 295 there is a sudden *crescendo*, followed by a precipitate descent to bar 301, the point of recapitulation. But this is no ordinary recapitulation. The effect is not so much of returning home as of running into a brick wall at speed. This is partly because the recapitulation arrives almost out of the blue; the *crescendo* of bar 295 comes far too late to prepare it properly. But it is also because of the major mode, in its unstable first inversion (with F♯ in the bass). Formally speaking, bars 301–20 correspond to bars 1–20; the effect, however, could hardly be more different. If the opening of the movement represents silence made audible, the recapitulation offers the most violently sustained *fortissimo* in the repertory. It is like a single *sforzando* that has somehow been spread over twenty bars, eventually subsiding out of sheer exhaustion.

By comparison with this, the remainder of the recapitulation takes a predictable course; in fact bars 357–426 correspond exactly to bars 88–157, transposed to D minor. And then begins the massive coda; as in the Third and Fifth symphonies, it makes up nearly a quarter of the movement's length. Moreover, it carries clear suggestions of being a second development, so opening up the bewildering possibility of an infinite movement in which expository and developmental sections alternate interminably with one another. It begins with a long *crescendo*, leading to the same dotted–note figure that concluded the first phase of the development (compare bars 188 and 463). And here comes the magical moment that Beethoven conceived six years before he completed the movement:[3] the passage for horns at bar 469, based on the first-subject figure that was used so much in the development, but now in the purest D major. This passage, too, has sometimes been heard as an anticipation of the finale; Vaughan Williams, for instance, called it 'a foretaste of the "joy" tune'.[4]

Further working of the first-subject figure, again reminiscent of the development, leads to a final feature shared with the Third and Fifth Symphonies. This is the striking new tune of bar 513, a kind of funeral march built over a grinding, chromatic ostinato. The ostinato is at first in the bass but it spreads upwards; by bar 525 it has taken over the entire registral range of the music. The movement concludes abruptly, with a fragmented statement of the first subject in massive octave doubling. The effect is oppressive and gnomic; the cloud cast by the funeral march is neither lifted nor explained.

As I have tried to suggest, the movement falls into and yet refutes sonata form. Because there is so little emphasis on D minor in the exposition, with the opening being in no clear key and the main theme moving rapidly towards B♭, the initial tonic is never really established. Beethoven dispenses with the symmetry of the traditional sonata plan. Instead, he creates a single tonal trajectory whose final destination is D minor. At the same time he creates a kind of large scale vacillation between D minor and D major. The most striking instance of this is of course the beginning of the recapitulation, at bar

301, where the opening of the movement returns in a shattering D major *fortissimo*. The previous hundred or so bars have centred on D minor and its neighbours; in this context the unprepared major mode sounds outlandishly dissonant. It also terminates a development that is, again unusually, the most relaxed section of the entire movement. This reversal of the normal tensional pattern of sonata form contributes to the effect that Kanne describes. Beethoven does violence to tradition; here is a source of the power and terror that Kanne heard in the music.

Second movement

The Scherzo section of this overwhelmingly extended and energetic movement is a complete sonata form in itself, in two repeated sections. The opening bars introduce both the dotted-note rhythm on which the Scherzo is based, and the timpani that play so striking a role in it. The main figure (bar 9) is first treated fugally, with entries four bars apart, building up to a homophonic climax at bar 57. Now the music moves from the D minor of the first subject area to an unconventional key for the second subject: C major, the key of the flattened seventh. A transitional passage on the dominant of the new key (bar 77) leads to the second subject proper, at bar 93. The music remains in C major until the end of the exposition, at bar 150.

The development begins with a vertiginous series of tonal motions by thirds, from D through B♭, G, E♭, C, A♭, F, D♭, B♭, G♭, E♭, C♭, A♭, E, and C♯ to A (bar 171), before rising by semitones to a fermata on B (bar 176). This leads to an extended fugal section, marked 'Ritmo di tre battute', in which the entries of the main theme are three bars apart; from bar 195 to bar 204 the timpani figure prominently, marking the first bar of each group of three. Bar 234 is marked 'Ritmo di quattro battute', suggesting that the conductor should revert to beating in groups of four, but in reality this is a *stretto*: the entries of the main theme are now only two bars apart. In tonal terms, the whole of bars 216–67 constitutes a prolonged dominant pedal in D minor, leading to the recapitulation at bar 272. A coda at bar 396 completes this section of the movement, which is linked to the Trio by a two-bar transitional passage (bars 412–13).

The basic design of the Scherzo seems to be based more on patterns of entries, as in a fugue, than on large-scale cadential structure; the most remarkable example of this is the end of the development section, which merges into the recapitulation without any trace of dominant harmony. The Trio (whose beginning is marked by the trombone's first entry in the entire symphony, at bar 414 – a moment that Mendelssohn always brought out when he conducted the work) is equally unconventional. It is in duple metre and consists of a series of variations in which the short, folk-like tune is repeated over and over again with different linear, harmonic, and orchestral accompaniments. These variations bear a striking similarity to the 'changing background' technique used by Glinka, and since the middle of the nineteenth century there have been repeated (though unsubstantiated) claims that the trio tune is in fact a Russian folksong.[5] The Trio is followed by a repetition of the Scherzo, conventionally taken without repeats, except that the original coda is replaced by a new and longer one (bar 531). At bar 549 it seems that the entire Trio is going to be repeated; just as in the first movement, there is a suggestion that the music will go on for ever. But the repetition falters after a few bars, and the second movement ends as abruptly as the first.

I do not find it easy to match what I hear with the responses of the 1824 critics. They were not struck by the imposing length of the movement, or by its raw dynamic energy. Instead they regarded it as playful and approachable, full of moment-to-moment detail. The *Theater-Zeitung* critic referred to the 'roguish comedy' of the Scherzo; the correspondent for the *Allgemeine musikalische Zeitung* said that in it 'The wildest mischief plays its wicked game . . . All the instruments compete in the banter, and a brilliant march in the major mode gives an unusual exhilaration to the contrasting section.' The trio struck Kanne in the same way; in it, he says, 'the ear at once regains new strength'. Despite the detail into which he enters, Kanne's response to this movement seems to have been as uncomplicated as those of his fellow-critics; from the start, he writes, 'The unusual tuning of the timpani . . . announces the humorous style', while the staccato runs in the woodwinds (he is probably thinking of the oboe solo at bar 454) make him think of 'the little Colombine tripping with her Harlequin, who springs in bold leaps from one modulation . . . to another'. Judging by their comments, this passage seems to have been a source of special delight for nineteenth-century listeners.

Kanne sounds only one note of reservation, and in doing so picks out one of the unusual formal features of the symphony. 'To us it seems almost a necessity', he says, that the agitation of the first movement 'be followed by the gentle, song-like, and melancholy Adagio, with the Scherzo being taken up later.'

Third movement

Kanne heard the Adagio as 'a most profound song, full of warmth, and flowing in heavenly melancholy'; the rest of his account, however, comments on specific details. He praises the figures in the winds at bars 7, 11, and so on, describing them as 'melting in graceful ecstasy like an echo'. He describes how the violins 'soar from the comfort-seeking sixth, still hesitatingly, to a higher tonal level, until they calm the spirit once again by bringing the tranquility that has long been withheld'; this is presumably a reference to bars 15–18. And he picks out the modulation at bars 23–4 which, he says, 'is not one of those in which many modern-day magicians break down the door of the house. On the contrary, it is sensitively realized.' Kanne's slightly barbed comment contrasts interestingly with that of the Parisian critic, François-Joseph Fétis, who complained a few years later that this same passage gave rise to 'a vague and indefinable sensation that results in fatigue rather than enjoyment'.[6]

Although he entered into some technical detail in his account of this movement, Kanne made no mention of the 'double variation' structure; few, if any, contemporary critics commented on it.[7] Admittedly it can be hard to hear this variation structure; at the slow tempo of the movement, the Adagio theme in B♭ is already long (bars 3–22, with 23–4 avoiding the cadence and preparing the new key), and it tends to get lost behind the violin figurations of the variations (bars 43–64 and 99–120). In any case, the variations occupy a relatively small part of the music. Between them come two Andante sections in 3/4 time, the first of them in D major (bar 25) and the second in G (bar 65). The form is also complicated by the episode from bar 83 (which begins as if it were a variation, but in E♭) and the long coda, which begins at bar 121 and is based on the Adagio theme together with a fanfare motif.

The result of all this is that the formal structure of the music is more obvious in the score than when heard. But then Kanne had seen the score. If he did not mention the way in which the movement is organized, this must be because he did not think it necessary or appropriate to do so. Insofar as one can extract a general principle from his review, and from those of other critics of the period, it is that technical commentary is useful to the extent, and only to the extent, that it allows the expressive content of the music to be grasped with greater precision than would otherwise be possible.

The other critics could do little more than express their admiration. 'What a heavenly song!', gushed the critic from the *Allgemeine Musikalische Zeitung*; 'what overwhelming transformations and combinations of motives; what artistic and tasteful development, how natural and yet sumptuous everything is; what grandeur of expression and splendid simplicity!' And as in the case of the first movement, the critic in the *Theater-Zeitung* resorted to metaphor. Beethoven, he wrote, 'leads us again into the deepest caverns of feeling, where the glittering gold of the soul glows in its purity; brightly shining gems give rise to thoughts of noble deeds in the future'. It is possible to read something more into this admittedly extravagant account than a diffuse response to the movement as a whole. The thoughts of noble deeds are presumably stirred by the curiously militaristic tones of bars 121–2 and 131–2; many subsequent commentators – among them Richard Wagner – echoed the *Theater-Zeitung* correspondent's response to these passages.

It is astonishing that none of these critics saw fit to comment on the extraordinarily complex and chromatic part for the fourth horn. Donald Tovey says that the fourth horn player in the first performance was the proud possessor of an early valved instrument.[8] This is an attractive suggestion, because it explains what otherwise looks like sheer perversity (why the *fourth* horn?). But there is no solid evidence for it, and the part is playable – with difficulty – on the natural instrument. Moreover, players of second (and fourth) horn parts tended to have highly developed hand-stopping skills; their parts lay in a lower register than those of the first (or third) horns, and they consequently made greater use of such techniques.

Fourth movement

Beethoven had difficulty describing the finale himself; in letters to publishers, he said that it was like his Choral Fantasy, Op. 80, only on a much grander scale. We might call it a cantata constructed round a series of variations on the 'Joy' theme. But this is rather a loose formulation, at least by comparison with the way in which many twentieth-century critics have tried to codify the movement's form. Thus there have been interminable arguments as to whether it should be seen as a kind of sonata form (with the 'Turkish' music of bar 331, which is in B♭ major, functioning as a kind of second group), or a kind of concerto form (with bars 1–207 and 208–330 together making up a double exposition), or even a conflation of four symphonic movements into one (with bars 331–594 representing a Scherzo, and bars 595–654 a slow movement).[9] The reason these arguments are interminable is that each interpretation contributes something to the understanding of the movement, but does not represent the whole story.

The key to the finale is the 'Joy' theme. It sounds as effortlessly natural as a folk song. But it gave Beethoven an enormous amount of trouble; there are literally dozens of versions of the last eight bars in the sketchbooks.[10] Now it was Beethoven's usual practice to map out the large-scale organization of his music before refining the melodic and harmonic materials. In this movement, however, he worked the other way round. Only when he had finalized the

Table 2 Ninth Symphony finale

Bar		Key	Stanza	
1	1[a]	d		introduction with instrumental recitative and review of movements 1–3
92	92	D		'Joy' theme
116	116			'Joy' variation 1
140	140			'Joy' variation 2
164	164			'Joy' variation 3, with extension
208	1	d		introduction with vocal recitative
241	5	D	V.1	'Joy' variation 4
269	33		V.2	'Joy' variation 5
297	61		V.3	'Joy' variation 6, with extension providing transition to
331	1	B♭		introduction to
343	13			'Joy' variation 7 ('Turkish march')
375	45		C.4	'Joy' variation 8, with extension
431	101			fugato episode based on 'Joy' theme
543	213	D	V.1	'Joy' variation 9
595	1	G	C.1	episode: 'Seid umschlungen'
627	33	g	C.3	'Ihr stürzt nieder'
655	1	D	V.1, C.3	double fugue (based on 'Joy' and 'Seid umschlungen' themes)
730	76		C.3	episode: 'Ihr stürzt nieder'
745	91		C.1	
763	1	D	V.1	coda figure 1 (based on 'Joy' theme)
832	70			cadenza
851	1	D	C.1	coda figure 2
904	54		V.1	
920	70			coda figure 3 (based on 'Joy' theme)

[a] *The second column of bar numbers refers to editions in which the finale is subdivided. Verses and choruses are numbered in accordance with the complete text of Schiller's 'An die Freude' (see Appendix 1)*

theme itself did he begin to give serious attention to matters of form. In fact what would conventionally be seen as an absolutely fundamental aspect of its formal structure, the move to B♭ major, only makes its appearance late in the sketches – after the finalizing of the 'Joy' tune, after the setting of the first three stanzas of the text, after he had decided to incorporate a variation in 'Turkish' style, and after the essentials of the 'Seid umschlungen' section had been worked out. Because of this, the best way to understand the movement is probably to chart the way in which it is built up from the 'Joy' theme.

Table 2 provides an overview of the whole movement and gives some idea of the way text and music are interrelated. We can begin with bars 208–330, which consist of three variations on the 'Joy' theme, together with an introduction. The introduction to this section is in D minor and consists of the initial *Schreckensfanfare* or 'horror fanfare', as Wagner called it, plus the baritone recitative that introduces not only the world of vocal music but the word 'Joy' (*Freude*) into the symphony. (The text of this recitative is Beethoven's, not Schiller's.) The variations, which begin at bars 241, 269, and

297, are settings of the first three stanzas of Schiller's *Ode to Joy*, and they build up from the baritone soloist to the full complement of four soloists plus chorus. They are in D major throughout, except that an extension to the third variation (bars 321–30) moves first to A major, the dominant of D, and then with a cataclysmic descent in the bass to F major in the final bar of the section – a move, incidentally, that unmistakably echoes the similar descent from F to D♭ in bar 133 of the third movement.[11]

If we take this section as our starting point, we can understand the rest of the movement by working backwards and forwards. The section up to bar 208 is essentially an instrumental version of bars 208–330, with an initial statement of the 'Joy' theme followed by three variations (bars 116, 140, and 164). It too begins with the *Schreckensfanfare*, and it is followed by two of the symphony's most famous features: the reminiscences of earlier movements (none of which is in fact a literal quotation), and the recitatives played by the cellos and basses. Nothing, perhaps, could form so effective a prelude to the introduction of voices as this dumb show, so to speak, in which instruments mimic speech. It is like a commentary on the thematic reminiscences, the words of which have been suppressed; in fact that is exactly what it is, for one of Beethoven's sketches for this passage actually assigns words to the recitative – words that were perhaps never meant to be sung, but provide a critical insight into what Beethoven had in mind at this point.[12]

The whole of bars 1–330, then, constitutes a massive block of D major, based on instrumental and vocal variations of the 'Joy' theme. This is followed by two further variations together with an extended fugato episode based on the 'Joy' theme (bars 343, 375, and 431 respectively). But at this point, for the first time in the finale, key structure begins to play an important role, for the 'Turkish' music beginning at bar 331 introduces a new key: B♭ major, the key of the second subject area in the opening movement. By aligning the keys of the first and last movements in this way, Beethoven creates at least a suggestion of sonata form in the finale. If we think of the B♭ as a contrasted tonal area, so that the 'Turkish' music becomes a kind of second subject, then the return to D for the final variation (bar 543) represents a kind of recapitulation, creating a quality of large-scale closure. Indeed the manner in which Beethoven handles the return to D major, over F♯ pedal notes in the horns (bars 517–40), creates a dramatic effect that is unmistakably borrowed from the sonata style. And the result is that, though based on a text, bars 1–594 create the effect of making up a more or less self-contained musical unit.

That can hardly be said of the section, or series of sections, between bars 595 and 762, which are not only based on a variety of new and disparate

36

musical ideas, but introduce a striking change in style. These passages set what Beethoven seems to have regarded as the core of Schiller's text: the choruses that affirm (but, as I shall later argue, perhaps also question) the existence of a loving Father above the stars. In setting them, Beethoven adopts a remote, hieratic style. The contours and modal inflections of the initial setting of 'Seid umschlungen' (bars 595–626) are clearly intended to evoke ecclesiastical chant, though by one of the ironies of reception history they can never sound to us like anything but Beethoven. At the same time, the large scale melodic and rhythmic momentum that has powered the movement up to this point seems to falter. As in the exposition of the first movement, the effect is of a daydream, or a series of daydreams. Each section comes to a halt on a fermata (bars 594, 654, and 762); at bars 647–54, where the repeated notes are surely meant to depict the twinkling of the stars, it is as if time stood still.

In this context the double fugue beginning at bar 655 represents a reawakening, a return to reality. It combines the 'Seid umschlungen' melody from bar 595 (now in D major) with the 'Joy' theme, in a manner that is perhaps closer to the world of Tchaikowsky's Fifth Symphony than to that of Haydn and Mozart. And it combines two formal functions. On the one hand, it concludes the section or sections that began at bar 595, providing some degree of integration between them and the remainder of the music; in fact it seems appropriate to revert to sonata terminology and describe the double fugue as having a recapitulatory function. On the other hand, it forms a transition to the coda, or series of codas, that begin at bar 763. From this point on, and despite some striking tonal and stylistic interpolations, the music never moves far away from D major. The final pages resemble nothing so much as an operatic finale, with a succession of short concluding figures more or less loosely derived from the 'Joy' theme, punctuated by two vocal cadenzas and a Maestoso passage (bars 810, 832, and 916 respectively) that hardly sound as if they had been written by Beethoven at all. I shall return to this in the final chapter.

As might be expected, the critics of 1824 showed no interest in the kind of formal issues that have exercised twentieth-century analysts. But they did not simply listen from moment to moment, as they seem to have done in the second and third movements; they grappled with what they saw as the real issues presented by the music. The critic in the *Theater-Zeitung* wrote the shortest account of the finale, but as in the case of the third movement his words sow the seeds of many later intepretations. 'The airy frame of instrumental music', he wrote, 'is no longer sufficient for the deeply moved artist. He needs to take the word, the human voice, to aid him so that he may express himself adequately. How will he express himself? What shall be his song? What else but a song of Joy!' Alone among these earliest commentators, the *Theater-Zeitung* critic explains Beethoven's decision to incorporate voices within his symphony in terms of the intrinsic limitation of instrumental music. In other words, he sees the introduction of the voices as a problem, or rather as the solution to a problem. This is the conception of the finale that the Berlin critic, Adolf Bernard Marx, set out in greater detail two years later, and we shall hear more of it in chapter 4.

The correspondent for the *Allgemeine musikalische Zeitung* contented himself with describing the unfolding of events in the finale, which he did with some style:

The finale, in D minor, announces itself like a crushing thunderclap, with a shrill, cutting minor ninth over the dominant chord. In short periods, as in a potpourri, the previously heard themes are all paraded before us in colourful succession, as if reflected in a mirror. Then the double basses growl a recitative that seems to ask: 'What is to happen next?' They answer themselves with a short, swaying motive in the major mode that develops as all the intruments gradually enter in wonderfully beautiful combinations, . . . building up, by measured gradations, into an all-powerful crescendo. Finally, after an invitation by the solo bass, the full chorus intones the song in praise of joy with majestic splendour. Then the happy heart opens itself up to a delightful feeling of spiritual enjoyment, and a thousand voices rejoice: 'Hail! Hail! to divine music! Honour! Praise! and thanks to its worthiest high priest!' – The critic now sits with regained composure at his desk, but this moment will remain unforgettable for him. Art and truth celebrate here their most glowing triumph, and with reason one could say: *non plus ultra*!

Up to this point, it is hard to imagine a more positive review. But the final comment – 'non plus ultra', no further – cuts both ways. And it is now that the critic introduces his only note of caution:

Who in fact could succeed in surpassing these indescribable moments? It is impossible for the remaining strophes of the poem (which are set partly for solo voices and partly for choral forces, in changing tempi, keys, and metres) to create a comparable effect, however excellently they are handled individually. Even the most glowing adherents and the most inspired admirers of this truly unique finale are convinced that it would be yet more incomparably imposing if it took a more concise form; and the composer would himself agree with this, if cruel fate had not robbed him of the ability to hear his creation.

These reservations, too, set a pattern for the future.

Kanne's review of the finale is in no way negative, but there is a distinctly polemical tone to it. He makes two basic points. The first concerns the originality of Beethoven's plan for the movement: 'one sees', says Kanne, 'how the world up to then seemed too small for him, and how he had to build himself an entirely new one.' But Kanne is at pains to distinguish the originality of Beethoven's forms from the superficial novelties of the 'newest composers' (he means the virtuosi like Thalberg), whose 'furious passagework' represents 'a striving for simple externals, for effects that are radiant but merely blind the inner sense of men'. These virtuosi, he says, have reduced music to gymnastics. In saying this, Kanne is associating himself with the classicizing reaction that I mentioned in the previous chapter. This becomes evident when he says, specifically in connection with the finale, that 'the composer's seriousness is shown in his strict control as he strives to imprint the stamp of classicism, by means of an organic interweaving of motives and a close attention to form. All of his phrases are connected with great thoughtfulness by chains of imitation.' This may be true, but it is hardly the most immediately striking feature of the finale. Kanne is clearly concerned to defend the Ninth Symphony, and Beethoven's late style in general, against the attacks that would soon be made upon it: that it was arbitrary, eccentric, and tasteless.

Kanne's other point is related to this. He sees the basic idea of the finale as being to unite the most heterogeneous, even contradictory, materials. As he says, it encompasses the themes of all the other movements with their distinct moods and metres; it includes recitative; it embraces the words of Schiller's Ode. (A twentieth-century critic might add that it also combines sonata, concerto, and four-movement symphonic form.) But, Kanne continues, even this is not enough for Beethoven; hence the introduction of the 'Turkish' music (bar 331). And here Kanne's discomfiture comes to the fore. Of course, he says, 'nobody would be so foolish as to assert that the composition is really in the so-called Turkish style. . . . For the authentically Turkish lies in the arbitrariness with which a composer erases all the artistic laws accepted by cultivated nations.' By contrast, he says,

Beethoven's oriental percussion orchestra is in accord with good taste . . . because he lets its increased powers enter only on highly accented beats and on characteristically meaningful syllables. His imagination is always in charge, not using it as a simple means of increasing the volume, but rather finding in it the realization of his rich, multi-faceted invention.

In other words, the Turkish music is not an alien element or a cheap piece of exoticism; it is absorbed within the organic structure of the music. Kanne is again attempting to secure the Ninth Symphony against criticisms of eccentricity and tastelessness.

Table 3 Some first performances of the Ninth Symphony

Vienna	7 May 1824	Umlauf
London	21 March 1825	London Philharmonic Society, Smart
Frankfurt	1 April 1825	Guhr
Aachen	23 May 1825	Ries (*Scherzo* omitted)
Leipzig	6 March 1826	Gewandhaus, Matthäi
Berlin	27 November 1826	Möser
Paris	27 March 1831	Société des Concerts, Habeneck
St Petersburg	March 1836	St Petersburg Philharmonic Society
New York	20 May 1846	Philharmonic Orchestra, Loder
Bandô camp (Japan)	2 June 1918	Performance by German POWs

The initial reception of the Ninth Symphony was warmer in Vienna than elsewhere, presumably because of Beethoven's personal prestige. As Table 3 shows, the symphony attracted a steady flow of first performances in the musical centres of Europe over the next few years. Everywhere these performances elicited the same criticisms that Kanne had sought to deflect. But nowhere were they voiced as stridently as in London. The story of the English reception of the Ninth Symphony is one of initial rejection gradually turning into adulation; it illustrates, in an exceptionally dramatic form, what happened in most of the cultural centres of Europe.

London, 1825–52

On February 1, 1825, soon after they had received their score of the Ninth Symphony, the Philharmonic Society of London held a public rehearsal, or 'Trial', of the work; the conductor was Sir George Smart. Two days later, *The Times* published the following notice:

A new symphony by the celebrated Beethoven was tried for the first time on Tuesday evening, at a rehearsal of the Philharmonic Society. In grandeur of conception, and in originality of style, it will be found, we think, to equal the greatest works of this composer. . . . The orchestra of the Philharmonic Society is in a state of great perfection, both in point of numbers and professional talent, and it could not have been put to a severer trial than in the execution, at first sight, of this noble composition by Beethoven.

If at first you don't succeed . . .

How well founded was the critic's claim about the orchestra's state of perfection? Sixty or seventy strong, it had a European reputation for the quality of its strings; the winds, however, were variable. A few years later, Henry Chorley compared the Philharmonic orchestra with the Société des Concerts de Conservatoire in Paris, which was conducted by François-Antoine Habeneck. In Paris, says Chorley pointedly, 'No unfortunate flute . . . chirps half a note before its time, – no plethoric bassoon drops one of its thick Satyr-like tones in the midst of a pause.'[13] As for the strings, he adds, 'you may see the phalanx of bows plying up and down on the strings with a mechanical consent and parallelism which in England can only be observed in those *fantoccini* orchestras that, under a monkey or a pair of white mice, borne by some black-eyed lank-haired Savoyard, loiter along those quiet streets where unfortunate literary men live'. And the reason for these differences? 'M. Habeneck has not, like our Philharmonic conductors, to give up his baton (I beg pardon, his violin bow), after his concert is over, to M. somebody else, who, for illustration's sake, may be as spirited as he is phlegmatic, or as phlegmatic as he is spirited.' The Philharmonic orchestra, in other words, had no permanent conductor.

But that is not all. It simply did not have a conductor in the modern sense. Through the 1820s and 30s, the Philharmonic orchestra operated under the system of dual leadership. This was essentially a hangover from the days of figured bass. The conductor, as he was billed, sat at a piano, filling in parts from time to time if he thought it necessary. He had a copy of the full score, but the actual marking of time was done by the leader of the orchestra, who used his bow, or his foot if he was too busy playing. And the leader, of course, had only the first violin part. Ludwig Spohr described this arrangement as 'the most topsy-turvy one imaginable', and put it down to native conservatism: 'the established thing is regarded here as holy and untouchable,' he said, 'the English in general . . . being the most wretched slaves to etiquette.'[14]

This dual leadership system was not the only thing that militated against Philharmonic Society performances. Another was the sheer length of the concerts: 'It is a mistake', wrote Ignaz Moscheles (who regularly conducted the orchestra during the 1830s), 'to give at every Philharmonic concert two symphonies and two overtures, two grand instrumental and four vocal pieces. I can never enjoy more than half.'[15] Worst of all, and despite the length of the programmes, only one rehearsal was allowed for each concert. The basic reason for this policy, which came increasingly under attack through the 1840s and 50s, must have been financial; the players had to be paid for each rehearsal, and potential income from the concerts was severely limited by the size of the Hanover Square Rooms, where the performances took place. The resulting manner of performance can be imagined. Wagner, who conducted the orchestra in 1855, wrote that 'The thing flowed on like water from a public fountain; to attempt to check it was out of the question, and every Allegro ended as an indisputable Presto. . . . The orchestra never played anything else but *mezzoforte*; neither a genuine *forte*, nor a true *piano*, came about.'[16]

It is not surprising, then, that the Ninth Symphony presented a severe trial to the orchestra. It evidently presented a severe trial to Smart, too. On 12 March, just nine days before the actual performance took place, he wrote in a letter to the Society that it would be much better if Beethoven could conduct the performance himself; 'for I have not the vanity', he continued, 'to imagine that I can fully enter into the ideas of the composer and, I candidly own, that I do not understand his meaning as to the style of the Recitative for the Basses, perhaps it should be play'd faster.'[17] And while the critic from *The Times* was clearly impressed by what he heard at the 'Trial', others shared Smart's reservations. The correspondent for *The Harmonicon* – possibly William Ayrton, its editor – complained about the symphony's length; it cannot, he says, last much less than an hour and twenty minutes. The same figure is also quoted in a highly critical review that appeared in *The Quarterly Musical Magazine and Review*.[18]

This critic complains that the opening of the first movement is indefinite; 'the basses and horns remain upon the two notes, E–A, . . . and form apparently a subject to work upon – but, like the Aurora Borealis, no sooner do you feast your eyes upon the phenomenon, that in an instant it vanishes from your sight.' (The rest of the movement, he admits, is masterly.) As for the Scherzo, he says, the style is brilliant, but 'I was not pleased sufficiently with the design of it to retain more than the first few bars.' But it is the finale that really upsets him. There are 'crude, wild, and extraneous harmonies'; there are 'odd and almost ludicrous passages for the horn and bassoon'. Worst of all is

the deafning boisterous jollity of the concluding part, wherein, besides the usual allotment of triangles, drums, trumpets, &c. &c. all the known acoustical missile instruments I should conceive were employed, with the assistance of their able allies, the corps of Sforzandos, Crescendos, Accelerandos, and many other os, that they made even the very ground shake under us, and would, with their fearful uproar, have been sufficiently penetrating to call up from their peaceful graves (if such things were permitted) the revered shades of Tallis, Purcell, and Gibbons, and even of Handel and Mozart, to witness and deplore the obstreperous roarings of modern frenzy in their art.

What, asks the critic, can have so upset the mind of the great Beethoven? His first answer is the obvious one: the composer, alas, is deaf. But he suggests another reason, and in so doing shows his true colours. The truth, he says, is that

elegance, purity, and propriety, as principles of our art, have been gradually yielding with the altered manners of the times to multifarious and superficial accomplishments, with frivolous and affected manners. Minds that from education and habit can think of little else than dress, fashion, intrigue, novel reading, and dissipation, are not likely to feel the elaborate and less feverish pleasures of science and art. . . . [Beethoven] writes to suit the present mania, and if this be so, he has succeeded in his purpose, for everywhere I hear the praises of this his last work.

This critic is not complaining that the finale of the Ninth Symphony is too difficult, obscure, or arbitrary. On the contrary, he is complaining that it is too *easy*; it has nothing to offer the connoisseur, but instead panders to fashion. The popular acclaim to which he refers actually counts against the work. In this wholesale assault on the taste of the times, there is more than an echo of Kanne's condemnation of the virtuosi whose furious passagework reduced music to gymnastics. Only this time the Ninth Symphony is arrayed on the other side of the battle lines. By stressing the organic unity of the finale, Kanne embraced it within the fold of the classical. The *Quarterly Musical Magazine* correspondent, by contrast, sees the Ninth Symphony as being in the vanguard of the noisy, tumultuous movement that we call Romanticism.

After the first performance proper, on 21 March, the critics from *The Harmonicon* and the *Quarterly Musical Magazine* saw no reason to change their opinions of the work, except that they both revised their estimates of its length to one hour and five minutes. (Smart punctiliously recorded the length of all the works he conducted; according to his records, the performance lasted one hour and four minutes.[19]) The *Harmonicon* correspondent seized this opportunity to lauch *his* attack on the finale. He says that it is

heterogeneous, and though there is much vocal beauty in parts of it, yet it does not, and no habit will ever make it, mix with the three first movements. . . . What relation it bears to the symphony we could not make out; and here, as well as in other parts, the want of intelligible design is too apparent. . . . In quitting the present subject, we must express our hope that this new work of the great Beethoven may be put into a produceable form; that the repetitions may be omitted, and the chorus removed altogether; the symphony will then be heard with unmixed pleasure, and the reputation of its author will, if possible, be further augmented.

And the critic from the *Quarterly Musical Magazine* ended his notice of the performance on a positively valedictory note:

The expence it entails in the engagement of a chorus, the necessity of repeated rehearsals, &c. &c. may perhaps forbid its ever being done again, and will certainly impede both its frequent repetition or its general reception. Yet it is the work of a great mind.

One has the distinct impression that these two gentlemen of the press felt that they had routed the Ninth Symphony. And, for the time being, they had.

. . . then try, try, and try again

The bare facts of the Battle of the Choral Symphony, as Adam Carse called it,[20] are quickly told. Smart visited Beethoven later in the year and talked to him, among other things, about the manner in which the instrumental recitatives in the finale should be played. Beethoven told Smart that at the Vienna performance they were played by four cellos and two basses; he also insisted – to Smart's surprise – that they must be played in strict time.[21] Armed with this new information, Smart persuaded the Philharmonic Society to attempt another 'Trial' of the work in 1828. But no performance resulted. Smart did, however, have a chance to put his ideas into practice two years later, at a private benefit concert; this time the performance lasted seventy-five minutes. But after that there were apparently no London performances until 1835, when the finale was included in a concert by the teachers and students of the Royal Academy of Music under Charles Lucas. By this time both *The Harmonicon* and the *Quarterly Musical Magazine* had ceased publication; the concert was well reviewed in *The Times*, which became something of a standard bearer for the Ninth Symphony over the next fifteen years.

The following year the Royal Academy performed the complete symphony. The success of this performance, together with a sustained press campaign by *The Times* and a new journal called *The Musical World*, stirred the Philharmonic Society into reviving the symphony. Between 1837 and 1851 the Society put on eight performances of it, at first under Moscheles, and subsequently under Michele (later Sir Michael) Costa; in 1837 they actually allowed *two* full rehearsals for it. Performance standards and critical response improved steadily throughout this period, especially after Costa was appointed permanent conductor in 1846. Though Costa personally disliked the symphony,[22] it was now becoming well known outside the Philharmonic Society: in 1841 the flamboyant Jullien featured the finale in his Drury Lane promenade concerts, replacing the solo singers by a choir of brass instruments. The symphony's position in the repertory was finally secured by a wildly successful performance under Berlioz in 1852, with the orchestra of the New

Philharmonic Society; this performance, said the following morning's edition of *The Times*, 'may fairly be presumed to have established the popularity of the ninth symphony'.

What were the factors that lay behind this dramatic reversal in the English reception of the Ninth Symphony? One of them, undoubtedly, was the improvement in performance standards. We can chart the progress in the wind players through the press reports. In 1838, *The Musical World* announced a forthcoming performance of the Ninth Symphony by the Philharmonic orchestra under Moscheles; it commented on the difficulty of the woodwind and horn parts in the third movement, and added that 'without being charged with temerity, we may therefore be excused the hint, that the symphony will go the better if the gentlemen who wield these instruments, were to look over their parts previous to the Monday's concert'. Nine years later things were not much better. On 30 March 1847 James Davison, who had just taken over as music correspondent for *The Times*, reviewed Costa's first performance of the work; 'most of the important points for the wind instruments were ruined by the performers', he said, as a result of their 'utter unacquaintance with the parts allotted to them in the score'.

Costa, who finally dispensed with the dual leadership system and used a baton, clearly got to grips with the problem. Just two years later, on 12 June 1849, Davison reviewed another performance under Costa: this time, he said, the third movement was

very finely executed with alternate delicacy and power, and the wind instruments were invariably in tune; the *obligato* passage for the third horn [he means fourth, or perhaps the part was reassigned] in the difficult key of G flat, about which the Paris Conservatoire is generally nervous, was rendered by Mr. Jarrett with the utmost neatness and purity.

And after another two years, on 8 April, 1851, Davison was writing that 'Every member of the band seemed bent upon doing his utmost, and we seldom remember Mr. Costa's pointed and decisive manner of "beating" more practically beneficial. In the *trio*, the oboe and bassoon parts, which are so prominent, were played to perfection.'

But one great problem remained: the allowance of only one rehearsal for each concert. 'The finale', Davison thundered in his 1847 review, 'should never be attempted without several careful rehearsals. To expect it to go satisfactorily with *one* would be too preposterous for any society but the London Philharmonic.' The Philharmonic Society remained unmoved, but Davison's words made their mark. Five years later the New Philharmonic Society was set up, in competition to the old one; it held its concerts in the much larger Exeter Hall, and its declared purpose was to present 'the greatest works by the greatest masters of all ages and nations'. The classical repertory, to which I referred in chapter 1, was beginning to solidify, and the Ninth Symphony already figured prominently in it. Indeed, the programme-book for the first series of concerts stated that one of the main aims of the new Society was to secure an adequate performance of this work.[23] The result was Berlioz's triumphant concert of 12 May 1852, for which an orchestra of 106 players was engaged. There were no less than seven rehearsals, including sectional rehearsals for strings and brass, and Davison's words from his 1847 review were printed in the programme note as a final slap in the face for the old Society.

Davison's predecessor at *The Times*, Thomas Alsager,[24] expressed his opinion about the Ninth Symphony over and over again in his reviews of the work: 'Its great characteristics', he said, 'are in fact simplicity and grandeur; only that the discovery was not made until it was perfectly executed.' But improved performance was not the only factor in the rehabilitation of the Ninth Symphony in England. It was tied up with the broad intellectual and artistic movement that we call Romanticism. I have already cited the way in which the *Quarterly Musical Magazine* correspondent, in 1825, associated the Ninth Symphony with novel reading and other kinds of dissipation. Three years later a critic calling himself 'Dilettante', writing in *The Harmonicon*, reinforced the association; he dismissed reports of the favourable reception in Berlin of 'Beethoven's worst, his most absurd work', on the grounds that 'A fanatical spirit is raging among a certain party of German amateurs, with a violence that tramples down reason, that treats the works of Haydn and Mozart as things gone by, and allows no merit but to noise, puerility, and extravagance.' The battle was essentially between eighteenth-century values based on taste and reason – values that seem to have survived for longer in England than elsewhere – and the Romantic ideal of personal expression. It was a collision of cultures.

What 'Dilettante', and others of his persuasion, saw as bad, the supporters of the symphony saw as good. In his 1847 review, Davison described the point of recapitulation in the first movement, with its sustained *fortissimo*, as 'appalling'. 'Dilettante' might well have agreed. But he would have understood this as a term of condemnation, whereas Davison intends it by way of praise. Again, Davison speaks appreciatively of the 'vague and indefinable feeling' created by the opening; the *Quarterly Musical Magazine* correspondent who compared it to the Aurora Borealis disliked it precisely because of this. And whereas the same correspondent was not sufficiently pleased with the Scherzo to retain more than its first few bars, the Beethoven partisan who wrote for *The Musical World* in 1838 evidently brought a quite different style of listening to the music: 'on what a bouyant sea of sounds does one seem to float', he declared; 'how vain the attempt to disentangle the maze of melodies – to single out, or to pursue through its labyrinths, the windings of any one in particular.'

In the rest of this review, and in a series of articles in subsequent issues, the *Musical World* critic provided, in effect, the Compleat Romantic's Guide to the Ninth Symphony. He emphasized the divine nature of Beethoven's creation, the fact that the composer followed the dictates of inspiration rather than writing to please his listeners, and the consequent need for dedicated and selfless study of the work. (Czerny's piano transcription of the symphony had come on sale two years earlier, in 1836, providing for the first time a means of easy access to the score.) When he speaks of the 'gorgeous colours' of Beethoven's music, or of the master's 'giant mind', his very language is redolent of the German Romantics. The critic from the *Quarterly Musical Magazine*, back in 1825, would surely have suspected him of reading novels and who knows what other dissipations.

In 1838, just thirteen years later, the time of 'Dilettante' and his cronies had decisively passed. The *Musical World* critic did not consider it necessary to address their views seriously. Instead he resorted to ridicule, contrasting the musical world they inhabited with Beethoven's – and, by implication, his own. He was particularly scornful of their assumption that they could judge a masterpiece of music such as the Ninth Symphony on a single hearing:

What notion could a gentleman who passes his life in filling up the thorough base of Mr. King's services, have of the scientific coating which envelopes the melodial phrases, and curious complications of harmony, to be found in the first movement of this symphony, from a single and excessively imperfect performance? What sympathy could the composer in the 'pure vocal school,' the arranger of old airs, or the gentleman whose gamut does not consist of more than twenty notes, have with the mind of a Beethoven . . .? Verily these personages did not understand a single passage of this great work; but the dark part of this singular story is, that they were not only content to remain uninformed, but actually gloried in their pharisaical and confined notions. But the force of public opinion has driven them from their entrenchments.

This account may be given in the guise of history, but it has the tone of myth.

3

Performance and tradition

The rise of the conductor–interpreter

In 1845, Moscheles addressed a few words to the musicians of the Philharmonic Society orchestra at the start of a rehearsal:

Gentlemen, as we are here assembled together, I should like to compare your performance with the fingers of an admirably trained pianoforte-player's hand. Now, will you allow me to be the hand which sets these fingers in motion, and imparts life to them? May I try to convey to you all the inspirations I feel when I hear the works of the great masters? Thus may we achieve excellence.[1]

In saying this, Moscheles was introducing a new, and distinctively Romantic, concept of the conductor's role; the conductor plays the orchestra as a virtuoso plays the piano, acting as an intermediary between composer and listener. Years later, Bruno Walter expressed the same idea in more overtly Romantic terms when he wrote that 'only he who understands that, under Wagner's baton, the *Ninth* sounded entirely in the spirit of Beethoven and that yet Wagner's own personality fully lived in it . . . comprehends the essence of musical interpretation.'[2]

And it is through Richard Wagner's eyes, and through his involvement with the Ninth Symphony, that we can best chart the rise of the conductor-interpreter.

Wagner the conductor

In the late 1820s, when he was in his teens, Wagner heard several performances of the Ninth Symphony at the Leipzig Gewandhaus. This was some years before Mendelssohn took over the orchestra; they played the first three movements under their leader, Heinrich Matthäi, with the conductor Christian Pohlenz taking up the baton for the finale. Like Smart, Pohlenz was clearly perplexed by the instrumental recitatives in the finale. Wagner describes a rehearsal.

Pohlenz conducted the fierce and shrieking fanfare with which this last movement begins in a cautious 3/4 time. . . . This tempo had been chosen to manage, in some way at least, the recitative of the bass intruments; but this never succeeded. Pohlenz sweated blood, but the recitative never came off, and I really began to wonder uneasily whether Beethoven had not written nonsense after all.[3]

What opened his ears to the Ninth Symphony, Wagner tells us, was hearing it played under Habeneck in 1839, while he was living in Paris.[4] It was 'as if scales had fallen from my eyes', Wagner wrote; 'in every bar the orchestra had learnt to recognize the Beethovenian *melody*; which plainly had escaped our brave Leipzig bandsmen of the time. . . . That glorious orchestra really *sang* this symphony.'[5]

Wagner's first opportunity to conduct the Ninth Symphony came in 1846, when he was *Kapellmeister* at the court in Dresden. The occasion was the annual concert given in support of the Royal Orchestra's pension fund.[6] As well as mounting a concerted publicity campaign to ensure the success of the performance, Wagner marked up all the orchestral parts, putting in his own indications of dynamics and articulation. As was common in performances of the Ninth Symphony, he used doubled winds; usually, he tells us, this was done in 'a rough and ready way . . . by having the parts marked *piano* played by a single instrument, and the parts marked *forte* played by both', but Wagner planned out the doubling carefully and wrote it into the parts. In addition to this, and no doubt remembering Pohlenz's experience with the instrumental recitative at the beginning of the finale, he held no less than twelve rehearsals for the cellos and basses. Fifty years later, Marie Heine, who was fourteen years old at the time, described how as a result of these rehearsals the cellos and basses played the 'Joy' theme 'with an evenness and tone volume giving the effect of the human voices; the theme itself murmured like an ideal inspiration, surging and fading until at last it joined the full orchestra with violins and violas'.[7]

The 1846 performance was a great success; it was repeated in 1847 and 1849. The next time Wagner conducted the symphony was in 1855, in the course of a season with the orchestra of the Philharmonic Society (who had no doubt engaged him in the hope of regaining the ground lost to the New Philharmonic Society under Berlioz). Like Moscheles before him, Wagner actually managed to wring two rehearsals out of the Society, and he was quite satisfied with the performance. The press reports, however, were mixed. George Hogarth wrote in the *Illustrated London News* that 'In regard to Wagner's character as an orchestral conductor, there was not on this occasion a single dissenting voice.'[8] But this was not true. Davison wrote that the first movement was 'all higgledy-piggledy', and that it was only by luck that 'the end was actually attained without a breakdown . . . The more closely we observe, the less we can understand him. He seems to have no fixed basis on which to found, no system to render intelligible, his manner of beating.'[9] At the end of Wagner's season, Davison pronounced that 'Herr Wagner has cut a sorry figure in this country, where plain common sense goes for something.'

The problem was that Wagner conducted in an essentially different manner from the kind of time-beating to which the London orchestras and critics had become accustomed in the 1850s. Anton Seidl described how 'the strange and significant movements of his long baton bewildered the players, and put them out until they began to understand that it was not the time-beat that ruled here, but the phrase, or the melody or the expression'. And this distinctive use of the baton, oriented towards the musical context rather than the barline, went together with a style of interpretation that was equally distinctive. Henry Smart, Sir George's brother and a violinist, complained of the way that Wagner 'prefaces the entry of an important point, or the return of a theme – especially in a slow movement – by an exaggerated ritardando; and . . . reduces the speed of an allegro – say in an overture or the first part of a symphony – fully one-third immediately on the entry of a cantabile phrase'.

Unfamiliar though they were in London, the ebbing and flowing of Wagner's tempos were not without precedent. Carl Maria von Weber (who was one of Wagner's predecessors at Dresden, and regularly visited the Wagner family home in Leipzig during Richard's childhood) was recommending a similar style of performance back in 1824:

The beat, the tempo must not be a controlling tyrant nor a mechanical, driving hammer. . . . There is no slow movement without places that demand a quicker motion in order to avoid a sense of dragging. In the same way, there is no Presto that does not require a contrasting, more tranquil, execution of many passages, for otherwise the expressiveness would be lost in excessive speed. . . . We have no way of indicating all this. It resides only in the feelings of the human heart, and if the feelings are not there, nothing is of any avail, neither the metronome, which serves only to prevent the grossest misunderstandings, nor the expression marks.[10]

Now much has been made of Beethoven's enthusiastic adoption of the metronome; he ascribed the success of the Berlin performance of the Ninth Symphony, under Karl Möser, to the fact that the performers had been supplied with metronome markings.[11] But Beethoven's approval of the metronome is no evidence that he wanted a metronomic unformity of tempo throughout a given movement. In fact there is ample evidence to the contrary. In the autograph of his song 'Nord oder Süd', he wrote '100 according to

Mälzel, but this applies only to the first measures, as feeling has its own tempo.'[12] And according to Ignaz von Seyfried, the music director at the Theater an der Wien, Beethoven's own conducting was characterized by rhythmic freedom: 'he demanded great exactitude in the manner of expression,' says Seyfried, 'minute nuances, the balance between light and shade, as well as an effective *tempo rubato*.'[13]

Most strikingly, we have what purports to be a transcription of one of Beethoven's orchestral performances, showing just such nuances. This is a twenty-one bar extract from the Larghetto of the Second Symphony, which Schindler included in the first edition of his *Life of Beethoven*.[14] Apart from dynamic inflections, we see a whole series of tempo modifications coordinated with the musical structure: if Schindler is to be trusted, Beethoven coupled *crescendi* with *accelerandi*, slowed down for *piano* passages, and reverted to the main tempo at structurally significant points. But *is* Schindler to be trusted? As Richard Taruskin has pointed out,[15] we have additional evidence on this point. Moscheles, who was personally familiar with Beethoven's style of performance, edited the English translation of Schindler's biography, and at this point he added a footnote. It reads: 'I agree with M. Schindler in these remarks. The slight deviations of time recommended must give life and expression not only to this movement, but also to the imaginative compositions of all the great masters.'

There is a strong case to be made, then, that Wagner's style of performing Beethoven had its ultimate source in Beethoven himself. And of all Beethoven's orchestral scores, there is hardly another that so strongly suggests a Wagnerian style of performance as the opening movement of the Ninth Symphony, with its profusion of *ritenuto*, *a tempo*, *cantabile*, and *espressivo* markings, its intricate use of dynamic indications and *sforzandi*, its radical contrasts of loud versus soft and high versus low, and its sheer proliferation of detail.

The letter and the spirit

Wagner's last, and most celebrated, performance of the Ninth Symphony took place in 1872, at the concert held to mark the laying of the foundation stone for the Bayreuth festival theatre. He assembled an orchestra of a hundred musicians drawn from all over Germany, and a chorus of three hundred. Special staging was erected in the Margraves' Opera House, where the performance took place, and – in apparent anticipation of *Parsifal* – two separate choirs of men's voices were positioned in the so-called trumpeters' boxes; they sang the initial *Seid umschlungen, Millionen* entry, creating an effect 'as if a mystery were being announced to the body of the chorus'.[16] Cosima Wagner noted in her diary that the performance was 'quite magnificent, everyone feeling himself freed from the burden of mortal existence'.[17]

Two subsequent publications give this performance its lasting significance. One is Heinrich Porges's documentation of it, which places particular emphasis on Wagner's use of *tempo rubato*.[18] From this we can reconstruct the basic outlines of Wagner's interpretation: the changing tempos of the opening movement, the rather slow Trio in the second movement, the extremely slow Adagio, the instrumental recitative at the beginning of the finale performed in strict time, and the very fast tempos in the final sections. The other publication to which the 1872 performance gave rise is an essay that Wagner himself published the following year, called 'The rendering of Beethoven's Ninth Symphony'.[19] In this, Wagner explained the changes to Beethoven's score that he had incorporated into the 1872 performance, and offered recommendations for further modifications. Out of the many modifications Wagner put forward, I shall discuss just two.

Wagner's retouchings

In bar 93 of the Scherzo, and again at bar 330, the main melodic line of the music is in the winds, with the strings having what is essentially no more than a dotted-note accompanying figure. 'I challenge any musician', says Wagner, 'to say with a clear conscience that he has ever plainly heard this melody in any orchestral performance.' The problem, as Wagner explains, lies in the balance between strings and winds. The horns and trumpets of Beethoven's day lacked valves, and so Beethoven was unable to deploy them to the full extent that was necessary if they were properly to counterbalance the strings. (Wagner's historical perspective is shaky here; performances in the 1820s and 30s did not use as many strings as Wagner had in 1872, but they often employed doubled winds, leading critics to complain that the wind band overwhelmed the strings.[20]) Up to now, Wagner says, he has tried to solve the problem by decreasing the dynamics in the strings, as well as doubling the winds. But this has never been successful. (Here Wagner contradicts himself; in 1867 he had said that these measures were entirely successful in the 1846 performance at Dresden.[21]) If he had to conduct this symphony again, Wagner concludes, he would not hesitate to add the horns to the melody line, and even bring in the trumpets if necessary.

Though Wagner never put these particular modifications into practice, they

52

were adopted by most subsequent conductors, remaining standard practice until around 1960. Hans von Bülow added the horns as Wagner suggested, but still found it necessary to mark down the strings; according to Walter Damrosch, who transcribed the markings in Bülow's personal copy of the score, he had them start *forte* in bar 93, but decrease to *mp* in bar 94, repeating the pattern thereafter.[22] Felix Weingartner, who published a detailed and highly practical essay called 'On the performance of Beethoven's symphonies' in 1906, considered Wagner's modifications indispensable, though he made minor changes to Wagner's horn parts; in fact he directed the horns to play *fortissimo* throughout.[23] Gustav Mahler's performance score, now at the University of Southampton, puts six horns and two trumpets onto the melody line.[24] Erich Kleiber, on the other hand, added just two horns, marking them *piano*.[25] And horns, in whatever numbers, can be heard in recordings by such conductors as Furtwängler, Walter, Klemperer, Ormandy, Stokowski, and even Toscanini, the advocate of playing music *com'è scritto*, as it is written.

Wagner's rationale for adding the horns in the Scherzo is fairly straightforward; the instruments of Beethoven's day were inadequate to the demands of the music, and so he wrote something that was plainly unsatisfactory. In adding the horns, we may violate the letter of his music, but we remain true to its spirit. But the second example of Wagner's modifications that I want to discuss is more complex, both musically and philosophically. It concerns the extraordinarily complex passage at bar 138 of the opening movement, sometimes called the third subject (Ex. 15). 'Who', writes Wagner, 'can declare that he has ever heard this passage, with distinct perception of its melodic content, at any of our orchestral performances?' Wagner proceeds to abstract what he sees as its essential melodic content (Ex. 16). Each two-bar phrase consists of a melodic descent; but, as Wagner sees it, Beethoven has confused this pattern by moving the flute into a higher register on the second semiquaver of bar 143, so obscuring the melodic contour. The solution, says Wagner, is for the flute to continue at the same register, as shown in Ex. 16. He also suggests that in bar 139 the oboe should play what is shown in Ex. 16, instead of omitting the G as Beethoven has it. Finally he adds dynamic nuances and recommends a slight slackening of the tempo at bar 138.

In the Scherzo, Beethoven was limited by the instruments available to him; here, in the first movement, he could perfectly well have written the passage as Wagner recommends, had he wanted to. So the rationale has to be that, whether through deafness or for other reasons, Beethoven did not succeed in writing what he meant in this passage; his *real* intentions are represented by Wagner's version, in which the essential melodic content emerges with proper

Ex. 15 First movement, bars 138-47

Ex. 15 (cont.)

55

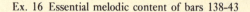

Ex. 16 Essential melodic content of bars 138-43

clarity. Dubious as this argument may seem, Wagner's modifications to bars 138–43 of the first movement were again widely accepted by later conductors. Weingartner adopted them all; these alterations, he wrote, 'without doing any detriment to the style, conduce to a clearness which cannot be obtained by means of a merely literal rendering'.[26] Mahler adopted them with further refinements. In the Southampton score, he changes the oboe part as Wagner suggests, and has the flute part played in octaves throughout. He eliminates the bassoons on the last crotchet of bar 143 and first semiquaver of bar 144, so as to bring out the beginning of the first bassoon's melody more clearly; he also has the second bassoon double the first at pitch. Finally he eliminates the trumpets and timpani, and reduces the *fortissimo* markings in the strings to *forte*. As for the evidence of recordings, Weingartner, Kleiber, and Bernstein shift the flute to the lower octave in bar 143; Toscanini, the purist, shifts it down from the previous bar.[27]

Whereas conductors readily adopted most (though not all) of Wagner's suggestions, there were always critics who deplored them as a matter of principle. Wagner, expostulated Sir George Grove,

seriously proposes to strengthen the melody in this place [Scherzo, bar 93] by adding horns and modern valve-trumpets, with other modifications. The wonder is that so great a composer should not have felt that *any* alteration of a completed work, by any but the author himself, is impossible. . . . Make the same proposition in regard to a picture or a poem and its inadmissability is at once obvious to everyone.[28]

Charles Gounod put forward the same argument: 'You do not redraw or repaint Raphaels or Leonardo da Vincis.'[29] And he continued:

I do not know Beethoven's Choral Symphony 'according to Wagner'; I only know it 'according to Beethoven', and I confess that that is enough for me. I have often heard and read this gigantic work, and in neither case have I felt that there is any need to correct it.

But a far more considered – if delayed – response to Wagner's alterations was made by the Viennese pianist and theorist, Heinrich Schenker, who published

Ex. 17 Third movement, bars 93-100 (Schenker)

an extensive monograph on the Ninth Symphony in 1912. Schenker's purpose in this monograph was to analyze the musical content of the Ninth Symphony, to offer recommendations for performance based on this analysis, and to refute erroneous interpretations of the work. As might be expected, Wagner figures prominently under the last heading.

Wagner and Schenker

Schenker does not deny that there is a problem of balance in bar 93 of the Scherzo.[30] But he insists that it is not a problem of Beethoven's making. In Beethoven's time, he says, the wind and string sections of the orchestra were properly balanced. The problem has been created by the modern orchestra with its inflated string section, and more generally by the demand that music be played to mass audiences in huge concert halls. The ideal solution, he continues, would be to return to the small orchestras of the past; but this is hardly likely to happen, since it would also mean a return to small halls and therefore a reduction in revenue.[31] So a solution has to be found. Wagner's solution, however, betrays a complete misapprehension of Beethoven's symphonic style. Beethoven used the horns as he did not because they couldn't play other notes, but because of 'the true nature of the horn, which, whenever it dominates at length (as is unfortunately so common today!), enfeebles the melody only too drastically as to both sense and sound'. Thus 'purely stylistic reasons alone compelled Beethoven to use the horns in exactly the way he actually did use them.' Hence the best solution is not to tamper with the wind parts; it is 'to introduce light and shadow into the *ff*', creating a kind of dynamic counterpoint between the winds and strings, as shown in Ex. 17.[32]

Schenker's complaint, then, is not so much that Wagner changes the notes; it is that, when he does so, he displays an inadequate grasp of Beethoven's music. And his refutation of Wagner's alterations to the passage at bar 138

Ex. 18

of the first movement follows similar lines. Like Wagner, Schenker approaches the passage in terms of its essential melodic content. I can clarify what is at issue by means of an analytical graph, using the reduction technique that Schenker himself developed and refined over the years that followed the publication of the Ninth Symphony monograph (Ex. 18). The lower two staves show the main melodic line and bass of bars 138–45; the beams show how each phrase is based on a scalar descent. The top stave picks out the boundary notes of each phrase, and shows that there is a strict sequential organization underlying the whole passage, with bars 142–5 repeating the pattern of bars 138–41 a third higher. This represents the melodic content of the passage in its most basic form, and these are the contours that Wagner wanted to bring out clearly; hence his alteration of bar 143 so that the flute completes its descent from d^3 to d^2.

Now Schenker's point is that so strong and regular an underlying structure as this does not *need* to be brought out with great clarity. It can speak for itself. That is why Beethoven orchestrates the passage in such a manner as to create variety and contrast. As Schenker puts it, the surface of the music camouflages its underlying structure; and this surface, with the shifting registers to which Wagner objects, is an intrinsic part of the musical expression. But, says Schenker, Wagner cannot not see this. His 'clarification-mania' betrays his unrefined musicianship; man of the theatre that he is, Wagner does not comprehend the subtleties of symphonic music.[33]

Because Schenker was aesthetically opposed to Wagner, and became more so as he grew older, we do not readily associate Schenker's way of thinking about music with Wagner's. And yet there are distinct similarities. Both Wagner and Schenker strip off the elaborations of the musical surface in order to arrive at the underlying melodic content. Or to put it another way, both think of music in terms of the relationship between surface and underlying structure. And more than that, Wagner strikingly anticipates Schenker's notion of diminution. The passage in which he does this is in the essay 'On conducting', which was written in 1869, and the music under discussion is once again the Ninth Symphony. Wagner is talking about the problem of determining the correct tempo. 'In a certain subtle sense', says Wagner,

one may say that the pure Adagio can not be taken slow enough. . . . Perhaps I am the only conductor who has dared take the Adagio proper of the third movement of the Ninth Symphony at a pace in strict accordance with its character. . . . The Adagio – particularly through the logical development given it by Beethoven in this third movement of his Ninth Symphony – becomes the basis of all measurement of musical time. In a delicately discriminating sense, the Allegro may be regarded as ultimate outcome of the pure Adagio's refraction by a busier figuration. If one takes a closer look at the ruling motives in the Allegro itself, one will always find them dominated by a singing quality derived from the Adagio. Beethoven's most significant Allegro movements are mostly governed by a root-melody, belonging in a deeper sense to the character of the Adagio.[34]

If Wagner's description of the song-like root melody underlying the figuration of the Allegro looks back to his account of Habeneck's orchestra 'singing' the Ninth Symphony, then equally it looks forward to the *Urlinie* of mature Schenkerian theory. It is hard to avoid the impression that Schenker derived some of his most basic concepts from Wagner's writings on the Ninth Symphony – even if he found the truth standing on its head in them, as Karl Marx did in Hegel.

In the same way, we have to understand Schenker's views on performance within the context of the Wagnerian tradition. To be sure, Schenker stands at the opposite wing of that tradition from Mahler, whose alterations of the Ninth Symphony approach full-scale recomposition. (For instance, Mahler consistently moves the tessitura of the clarinet and bassoon parts upwards, filling in the resulting gap by means of the enlarged horn section; the result is a distinctively Mahlerian tone quality.) Conductors like Klemperer admired Mahler's retouchings, but they did not adopt them; they considered them too personal.[35] Again, Weingartner attacked the 'distortions' that had become commonplace in the performance of Beethoven's symphonies, insisting that the notes should be changed 'only in the very rare cases in which there was absolutely no other means of obtaining the effect which Beethoven wanted to produce'.[36] But these 'rare' cases turn out to include most of Wagner's alterations.

Despite this, Schenker's position is not so far removed from Weingartner's. Weingartner recommends the kind of detailed marking-up of parts that Wagner did at Dresden; Schenker approves. Schenker praises Weingartner's suggestions for dynamic shading at bar 301 of the first movement – shading which is also found in Mahler's version. To be sure, Beethoven does not indicate any such shading. He simply marks everything *fortissimo*. But, says Schenker, the shading is musically necessary; Beethoven assumed that the conductor would supply it. The difference between Weingartner and Schenker is that Schenker is prepared to go to almost any lengths to avoid changing the actual notes. (Our loyalty to Beethoven, he says, demands this.) But when he sees no other choice, he is prepared to change them. In bar 758 of the finale, he writes, 'Beethoven seems to have suffered a lapse'; the clash between the C♮ in the winds and the C♯ in the alto and viola parts is impossible, and the wind parts must be changed accordingly.[37] There is no attempt to argue that the text has somehow become corrupt; the change is made solely on the grounds of the musical content. Like Wagner, Schenker is telling us what Beethoven *really* intended. The principle is the same.

If we locate Schenker firmly within the Wagnerian tradition of performance, then we can see his monograph on the Ninth Symphony as providing a grammar of nuance as it was understood within that tradition. He begins his comments on the performance of the first movement by emphasizing that Beethoven's metronome marking applies only to the opening; by no means, he says, does it rule out subsequent tempo modifications. And he specifies a substantial number of these modifications, in each case explaining why the musical context demands it. Here are some of them. Around bars 94–5, says Schenker, the *crescendo* (actually marked in bars 92–3) should be coupled with a *stringendo*, with a compensating hesitation at the beginning of bar 96, where the dynamic falls to *piano*. At bar 138, and in the following bars, the tempo should be imperceptibly held up at the second or third semiquaver, so as to bring out the rising motive in the melody; in bars 145–6 there should be a minute acceleration to underline the progression from subdominant to dominant. At bar 154, with the telescoping of the dotted-note figure, an *accelerando* should begin, so as to 'reflect in the medium of time that quality of compactness that has built up in the medium of the motivic'.[38] Similarly, from around bar 449, there should be a *stringendo* to contribute to the breaking up of the four-bar phrase structure. Other tempo modifications are dictated by the large sections into which the movement falls.

Furtwängler, Toscanini, and authenticity

What would all this have sounded like? The best answer is to listen to one of Wilhelm Furtwängler's recorded performances of the symphony. Furtwängler read Schenker's book on the Ninth Symphony and was so impressed by it that, in 1919, he started taking private lessons with Schenker. Ten years later, Schenker heard one of Furtwängler's performances of the Ninth Symphony and noted in his diary that it was 'much better than before, though the Adagio dragged and there were other small errors'.[39] To be sure, Furtwängler's recordings (all of which are taken from live concerts) incorporate elements of which Schenker would not have approved, such as the horns in the second movement. But they also incorporate tempo modifications like those Schenker recommended. The best known recording was made in 1951, at the opening of the first Bayreuth Festival to be held after the war; it was a self-consciously historic occasion, with overtones of Wagner's 1872 performance.[40] Most, though not all, of the nuances that Schenker describes in the first movement can be found in this recording. But to call them nuances is perhaps misleading. It is not simply a question of bringing out moments. Entire sections are underpinned by changing speeds; an astonishing example of this is the sustained *accelerando* from bar 427 to bar 452 of the first movement. What Furtwängler offers is a fully mobile tempo, closely coordinated with the musical design. It is in this sense that, as Peter Pirie says, 'His interpretation analysed the structure.'[41]

Like Wagner, Furtwängler was accused of not having an intelligible beat. (In the Berlin Philharmonic they had a joke: *Q.* How do you know when to come in on the opening bars of the Beethoven Ninth? *A.* We walk twice around our chairs, count ten and then start playing.[42]) The reason was the same: he beat in phrases rather than bars. The leader of the Berlin Philharmonic, Henry Holst, put it like this:

His beat lacked that 'flick of decisiveness' that will enforce precision over an ensemble. That kind of precision he did not like at all: he wanted the precision that grew out of the orchestra, from the players' own initiative, as in chamber music.[43]

When Holst referred to the 'flick of decisiveness', he may well have been thinking of Arturo Toscanini, whose conducting was widely seen as the antithesis of Furtwängler's, and who was more than anybody responsible for, if not the demise, then the dilution of the Wagnerian tradition of performance to the point that it no longer carried conviction. Toscanini, whose orchestral discipline was legendary, came from a background in Italian opera, and brought a streamlined, unfussy approach to the German symphonic repertoire; he was, so to speak, the Stravinsky of the classics. He also brought a vociferous (and again Stravinsky-like) insistence that everything that mattered about music was in the score; all that was necessary was to play it as written, *com'è scritto*. By the end of his life he had established an orthodoxy of interpretation. Paul Henry Lang, who for many years edited *The Musical Quarterly*, was an influential record critic as well as a prominent musicologist, and in 1971 he published an overview of the available recordings of Beethoven symphonies. He wrote:

Toscanini burst upon a musical scene dominated by sentimental German (and German-trained) conductors, more interested in 'expressive interpretation' than in stylistic faithfulness, orchestral discipline, and precision. . . . Toscanini's verve, integrity, strict adherence to the score, and unparalleled demands on the orchestra established new standards for ensemble playing, dynamics, tempo, and so forth, which almost totally changed the art of orchestral playing. . . . He does not miss a single comma in the score, he scorns unauthorized pauses, and his crescendos are carried out with minute attention to dosage.[44]

What, then, did Lang think of Furtwängler's recordings of the Ninth Symphony? The answer is perhaps predictable. Lang speaks first of the wartime recording Furtwängler made with the Berlin Philharmonic:

The allegro is played at a constantly variable speed; the scherzo, believe it or not, is too fast, but the trio is nice and at the correct tempo. The adagio is so slow that it turns into aspic. The bass recitatives in the finale are like Liszt rhapsodies . . . The 'Turkish' music with the tenor solo just flips along, the fugue is fantastically fast and inarticulate, the choral portions get by. . . . [The 1951 recording], with the Bayreuth festspielhaus forces, is something of a treasured antique, though I can't see the reasons for the admiration. The performance is somewhat better. . . . In the allegro the tempo does not fluctuate so much, the scherzo is not so hard-driven, the adagio is less agonizing, and the finale is much more reasonable in tempo and articulation. But Furtwängler insists on giant fermatas, and the pauses after them are so long that the unwary may think that the end of the side has been reached.[45]

Lang characterizes Furtwängler's performances in wholly negative terms: they are tolerable to the extent that the tempos don't fluctuate, the Scherzo doesn't go too fast, the slow movement doesn't go too slow, and so on. More than anyone, it was Lang who gave musicological credibility to the idea that Beethoven's music, and classical music in general, should be performed in a 'steady and relentless tempo', as he put it; he quoted statements to this effect by late eighteenth-century writers. Now one might question how relevant late eighteenth-century views are to music written in the 1820s. But that is not the only respect in which Lang's argument is questionable. In his recent article on the Ninth Symphony, Richard Taruskin has demonstrated that Lang took his quotations out of context to the extent that he completely misrepresented what they were saying. The writers he quoted were in fact advocating just the kind of tempo modification that Lang condemned. It seems to have been a classic instance of fixing the evidence to suit a preconceived opinion. Lang spoke of 'stylistic faithfulness' to the classics; what he was really doing, like Toscanini, was imposing a modernist aesthetic upon them.

Lang referred to Toscanini's 'strict adherence to the score', but in fact Toscanini did not play the music as written. He introduced pauses that weren't in the score. He adopted most of Weingartner's alterations in the Ninth Symphony. And as a result, he was sometimes criticized by his own adherents, who took his maxims more seriously than he did; Spike Hughes, for instance, complains bitterly about the dynamic shading that Toscanini gave to each of the long notes in bars 120–27 of the first movement[46] – shading that is not to be seen in Beethoven's score, but could be found in the performances of Bülow, Weingartner, Mahler and Furtwängler. (It can also be found in Nikolaus Harnoncourt's recording, released in 1991.[47]) For a thorough-going observance of Toscanini's maxims, we have to look not to Toscanini's recordings, but to those recently issued by Roger Norrington and Christopher Hogwood.[48]

Both conductors set great store by the observance of Beethoven's metronome markings, and the results can be startling. They take seriously the notated tempo for the Trio in the second movement, minim = 116, which other conductors have long rejected as impossibly slow. They play the slow movement at nearly Beethoven's marking (crotchet = 60); Furtwängler took it at half this speed. And in the finale, they take the whole of the section beginning with the 'Alla Marcia' (bars 331–594) at something approaching the dotted crotchet = 84 that Beethoven marks in bar 331. The last of these is perhaps the most far-reaching in its consequences. As Norrington puts it in the sleeve notes to his recording, 'the steady, homespun, "villagey" pace has a humour and a humanity about it which is very important to the movement. . . . Beethoven's message is for all men, not just for heroes. *"Alle menschen werden Brüder"*, both the sublime and the beery.'

Now this is a perfectly logical interpretation of the finale; in fact there seems to be something of an English tradition of interpreting it this way.[49] But it cannot really be said to be more historically justified than the rapt, mystical religiosity of Furtwängler's. Even if Beethoven did intend the opening of this section as dotted crotchet = 84, but what evidence do we have that he expected this tempo to be adhered to throughout the following 263 bars of extremely diverse music? Isn't it another case of the metronome marking applying 'only to the first measures, as feeling has its own tempo'? The question cannot be settled on the basis of *com'è scritto*, because what is at issue is the interpretation of what is written. In fact it's hard to see what kind of evidence *could* settle the issue conclusively. If these aggressively literal interpretations carry conviction, then, this must be on musical grounds, not musicological ones.

'We play the score as it stands', says Norrington, 'without any rewriting, additions, or doubling of wind or brass.' Doubled winds would be completely inimical to the very special sound quality that Norrington creates. But then, doubled winds were used at the first performance. (Even Hogwood uses them.) In this way, when Norrington writes that 'we want to restore this Ninth Symphony to the humane, quicksilver thought-world of the Classical Period', he is situating the symphony in a context to which it never really belonged in the first place. In fact, to the extent that the historical performance movement aims to recreate the conditions of early performances, there is something distinctly paradoxical about aiming for authenticity in performing the Ninth Symphony. *Which* early performance might we want to recreate? The first one, in the Kärntnerthor Theater, with Umlauf sharing the direction with Schuppanzigh and possibly Beethoven as well, with the violinists setting down their bows when the music got too hard and the sopranos falling out when their parts got too high? Or the disastrous English premiere under Sir George Smart? Or Berlioz's 1852 performance in London? Or Wagner's 1872 performance at Bayreuth?

The Ninth Symphony achieved lasting success in performance only after the dual leadership system had been swept away and the modern conductor had taken over. It is, in this sense, a work of the Romantic repertory. The attempt to restore it to the Classical Period is in reality an attempt to appropriate it for the late twentieth century, in disguise.

4

The Romantic Ninth

Interpretation and appreciation

In 1896, an anonymous critic voiced his reservations concerning the opening of the Ninth Symphony in the *Edinburgh Review*.[1] He complained of 'the rather eccentric and certainly not happy device of anticipating the real subject by the weak and uninteresting tentative passage, as it may be called, which mystifies the hearer at the opening. . . . How far grander and more impressive would have been the immediate starting off with the broad and powerful unison passage which forms the real theme of the movement!' But Antony Hopkins could not disagree more. He says:

I doubt whether in all music there is so profound a statement expressed in fundamentally simple terms as we find here. . . . Suspense is prolonged with masterly skill so that when the final release into D minor does arrive its force is intensified to an extraordinary degree. . . . Just as a tidal wave gathers its force invisibly, far out to sea, so this gigantic theme coils itself from a deceptively suppressed opening chord before unleashing its awesome ferocity upon us.[2]

It is not simply that the two writers hear the same music but judge it differently. It is as if they were not hearing the same music at all. In the face of such contradictions, it is tempting to conclude that people's responses to music are irremediably subjective: one person hears it one way, the next hears it another way, and that is an end to the matter.

Interpretation and the listener

But this is not the whole story. People can be influenced in the way they hear music. And this means that traditions of listening grow up. I can illustrate this in terms of British responses to bar 301 in the first movement of the Ninth Symphony, the beginning of the recapitulation. Writing in 1896, Grove heard this passage – a sustained *fortissimo* in which the opening of the movement returns in D major – as a triumphant assertion: 'Instead of that vagueness and mystery which made it so captivating, it is now given with the fullest force of the orchestra and the loudest clamour of the drum. . . . Its purpose is accomplished, its mission fulfilled, its triumph assured; no need now for concealment or hesitation!'[3] And Edwin Evans, whose detailed analyses of Beethoven's symphonies first appeared just before the First World War, heard the recapitulation the same way; according to him, it expresses 'courage, ardour, hopefulness, fortitude'.[4] He adds: 'Never was there a return so significant as this; for, with incoming of the minor [he is referring to bar 315], shouts of triumph are changed into those of determination to continue the struggle.' It is tempting, and I think legitimate, to read into these interpretations the martial values of the British Empire.

But when Donald Tovey published his analysis of the Ninth Symphony, between the two world wars, he wrote about this passage in very different terms. He calls it a 'catastrophic return', and explains what he means in detail:

Hitherto we have known the opening as a pianissimo, and only the subtlety of Beethoven's feeling for tone has enabled us to feel that it was vast in sound as well as in spaciousness. Now we are brought into the midst of it, and instead of a distant nebula we see the heavens on fire. There is something very terrible about this triumphant major tonic, and it is almost a relief when it turns into the minor as the orchestra crashes into the main theme.[5]

Like Grove and Evans, Tovey hears the passage as triumphant; but for him the triumph is threatening, destructive, inhuman. His talk of the heavens on fire brings to mind the air raids of the second world war – though Tovey could not, of course, have been thinking of them. But those who read Tovey's words after the war may well have done so. Maybe that is why Tovey's interpretation of this passage affected them so deeply; British critics of the generation after Tovey barely stopped short of plagiarism when they wrote about this passage. Basil Lam likens the music to a 'flame of incandescent terror'.[6] Robert Simpson speaks of the 'flaming supernova explosion of the reprise, in a terrible D major. . . . We glance at the sky – and it is blazing from horizon to horizon. We are flung into the heart of the fiery D major nebula, and the recapitulation has begun.'[7]

Whereas Simpson reduplicates Tovey's images – the sky on fire, the nebula – Antony Hopkins substitutes a new one of his own. But the emotional tone of his interpretation is very like Tovey's:

One might expect the emergence of a major key into this context to induce a feeling of optimism or even triumph, yet such is the character of the theme that it cannot do so. It is awe-inspiring in the same way that a vision of the avenging angel would be; one's eyes would be dazzled by his radiance though one's heart would quake with terror.[8]

Hopkins regards his interpretation as self-evident: such is the character of the theme that it 'cannot' induce a feeling of optimism and triumph. Yet optimism and triumph are exactly what Grove and Evans heard in this passage. This shouldn't occasion too much surprise. When people have come to hear a piece of music in a certain way, they generally find it difficult to hear it in another way, or even to imagine that there could be another way of hearing it.

Tovey just asserted his interpretation; he did not really try to explain or justify it. But the American critic, Leo Treitler, has tried to do this. He agrees with Tovey that the beginning of the recapitulation creates a sense of catastrophe. 'But why?', he asks. And he replies: 'It is the shock of *fortissimo* where we had known *pianissimo*, of the full orchestra where it had been the strings alone . . . , of the full triad where it had been hollow fifths, of D major when the preceding four measures had been preparing D minor. . . . It is, all in all, the shock of being now pulled into the opening with great force, instead of having it wash over us.' Or, to put it another way, it is the contrast between the manner in which the opening of the movement steals in ('it is as though the music had always been going on, but the volume is just now turned up') and the explosive irruption of the recapitulation. For Treitler, the first bars of the Ninth Symphony adumbrate a new kind of musical time that is 'circular, in contrast to the progressive or dialectical time that is the essence of the Classical sonata procedure'.[9] And it is this new conception of time, he argues, that is responsible for the sense of the cosmic and infinite which so many listeners – Tovey included – have sensed in the work.

This brings us back to the critic in the *Edinburgh Review*. He tried to hear the opening of the Ninth Symphony in terms of the Classical conception of time to which Treitler refers and so found himself, long after the music had started, still waiting for it to begin properly. Modern listeners, by contrast, have learnt to hear the opening in terms of a kind of sustained timelessness; hence the masterly prolongation of suspense to which Hopkins refers. In the opening as in the recapitulation, then, a tradition of hearing the Ninth Symphony has grown up. And a measure of the significance of critical interpretation is the power that Tovey had to mould the way in which a generation of listeners heard Beethoven's music.

Creating meaning out of incoherence

The *Edinburgh Review* critic of 1896 seems to have stepped out of the era of *The Harmonicon* and the *Quarterly Musical Magazine*. He complains of the 'earnest tone' which pervades the music, and its 'want of spontaneity and charm'. He describes the instrumental recitative in the finale as 'a piquant piece of musical humour, but . . . much overrated'. And he ends by excusing the excesses of the finale on the grounds of the composer's deafness. It is as if Romanticism never reached Edinburgh.

It was the arrogance, or what they saw as arrogance, of Ayrton and the other writers in *The Harmonicon* and the *Quarterly Musical Magazine* that particularly infuriated Romantic critics. Even the normally placid Grove refers to them as 'gentlemen who were not only far behind the great composer whom they were criticizing, but believed themselves to be so far his superiors as even to advise him how to modify his work that it might obtain their approbation'.[10] But what Grove saw as arrogance was really the product of an aesthetic attitude that Romantic critics did not share. In true eighteenth-century manner, Ayrton and his colleagues believed that music should please the senses and avoid unnecessary complication; as the Beethoven fanatic who wrote in *The Musical World* put it ten years later, they wanted everything set down in such a manner

that it might be intelligible at half a glance. Beethoven, however, places his drums here, his bassoons there, and double basses in another situation, purposely to arrest attention, and excite reflection. Now, our artists were then too much in the habit of frequenting the concert room, not to learn, but to decide.

Reflecting upon the music, learning from its problematic features: these are Romantic attitudes. They are based on the idea that the composer's primary duty is to be true to himself, and that listeners must be prepared to invest time and effort in coming to an understanding of what he has written. Perhaps the most striking expression of these values comes from a correspondent of *Dwight's Journal of Music*, signing himself as 'P', who filed a report on Berlioz's 1852 performance of the Ninth Symphony in London.[11] 'Being the first time I had ever heard this mighty work of art,' he writes, 'I hardly dare to say what my impressions were.' Nevertheless he provides descriptions of the first three movements. 'Then came the last movement,' he continues,

about which I stay my pen. I did not understand it, and reverently stand in hope and faith, that its secrets may at some future day be revealed to me. It is acknowledged even by those who know it best, to be the most obscure of Beethoven's productions, the most difficult to be understood; and it would be folly to try even to form one's thoughts upon it after a first hearing.

A greater contrast with the attitude of the critics from *The Harmonicon* and the *Quarterly Musical Magazine* could hardly be imagined.

As we have seen, Romantic attitudes became established earlier in Germany than in England. Prior to the first Berlin performance of the Ninth Symphony, in 1826, Adolph Bernhard Marx published a series of articles in the *Berliner allgemeine musikalische Zeitung*. These articles were designed to prepare the music-loving public for the event, and in one of them Marx sets out something like a rationale of music appreciation. His starting point is the priority of the artist over his audience.

It is the artist in whom the first impulse to creation rises, in whom the idea of inspired passion and penetrating meditation matures, nourished by the noblest powers, perfected and realized in the fullness of time. How can the receiving public, without authentic artistic calling, without preparatory schooling or practice, without the same orientation, without a developed perception, and by way of recreation rather than the highest spiritual concentration – how can such a public fancy itself to be called upon to judge an artistic work? How can they think themselves competent to dispose, in an hour or two, of something that cost a talented artist the best years of his life? . . . One should seek causes for the failure of an artwork to make a good impression in oneself, not in the work. One should not turn away from what is at first incomprehensible or repugnant, but instead diligently follow the artist's progress.

Having thus set out what he sees as the proper relationship between composer and listener, Marx lays down some guidelines for appreciating the Ninth Symphony. He chooses as his starting point precisely the aspect of the work that listeners and critics found most problematic.

Anyone who thinks of this creation of Beethoven's as a vocal composition in the normal sense will inevitably find it incomprehensible and imperfect: incomprehensible in that there is so long an introduction (four [*sic*] large symphonic movements) to a moderately long cantata; imperfect as regards the setting – or rather the breaking up – of the poem.

But at this point Marx gives the argument an unexpected twist: in view of all this, he says, 'we must recognize that it is something other than a vocal composition'. Instead of seeing the finale as a 'casual closing chorus', Marx sees it as the essential element in a single musical process that encompasses both the purely instrumental world of the first three movements and the synthesis of instrumental and vocal music in the finale. The progression from the one to the other, he says, symbolizes man's triumph over nature: 'As soon as the instruments and voices come together, the former subordinate themselves to the latter, just as everything that surrounds man does to him; because in song, which embraces speech and the world of tones that dwells in man, the human is portrayed, whereas instruments portray the non-human.' Even the deficiencies of the text setting, considered from a conventional point of view, are turned to advantage in Marx's interpretation: Beethoven 'let the voices go their own way so that they could be, so to speak, victorious in their own right, even without any care on the composer's part as to the declamatory, melismatic, or harmonic aspects of the melody.'

Whether by chance or because he had read it, Marx's interpretation builds on the review of the first Vienna performance by the *Theater-Zeitung* critic, who spoke of Beethoven's need to move beyond the limitations of instrumental music.[12] But the *Theater-Zeitung* critic said this merely in the context of the finale. Marx takes the idea much further by making it the basis of an integrated interpretation of the whole symphony. In doing this, he seeks to preempt the criticisms of conservative critics by showing, as Robin Wallace puts it, that there is 'no need for unity; the second half of the symphony simply transcends the first half, which takes on the character of an introduction'.[13] Marx creates narrative links between the diverse elements of the music; he inserts his message into the gaps between them. In short, he creates meaning out of apparent incoherence.

Much the same can be said of Franz Joseph Fröhlich, who wrote a review of the symphony for the Mainz-based journal *Caecilia* in 1828.[14] A professor at Würzburg University as well as a practical musician, Fröhlich began by explaining how he had at first been sceptical about the work. 'Only after careful study of the score,' says Wallace, did Fröhlich 'become convinced that it was an aesthetic whole: that indeed it was the greatest symphony ever written.' For Fröhlich, the key to understanding the Ninth Symphony lies in identifying the basic idea behind the music: the power of joy to overcome sorrow. This is made explicit in the words of the finale, Fröhlich says, but it is implied in the first three movements, which have to be understood in a narrative and autobiographical sense. The first movement depicts Beethoven's struggle with deafness; the second and third movements represent different aspects of his quest for joy. And the final success of this quest is symbolized by the large-scale motion of the symphony from D minor to D major. Understood in these terms, Fröhlich says, the Ninth Symphony has an essentially simple structure.

Nowadays we take it for granted that the Ninth Symphony's motion from D minor to D major is significant. In fact Ernest Sanders says that 'It is a truism that the basic "thesis" of the Ninth is the victory of tonic major over tonic minor.'[15] But it was not always so; according to Wallace, Fröhlich's review represents the first time that such an idea had been put forward in the context of any multi-movement work. Other aspects of Fröhlich's interpretation, however, echo Kanne's review of the first two performances, which I discussed in chapter 2. Both Kanne and Fröhlich construct literary analogues of the music, expressing the same ideas, but in words instead of notes. Both think of the music in autobiographical terms: they see the struggles depicted in the first movement as Beethoven's struggles, though only Fröhlich extends this idea to the symphony as a whole. And again like Kanne, Fröhlich goes into musical details just to the extent that they elucidate the narrative or emotional content of the music. For instance, he explains that bars 1–16 of the first movement represent tender longing, bars 17–20 heroic strength, the following bars tragic pathos, and bars 28–30 the perception of joy itself. Taken together, says Fröhlich, these make up the portrait of an uncommonly powerful personality, that of Beethoven himself; they set out the basic material of the whole movement in both a technical and an emotional sense.[16]

Between them, Fröhlich and Marx established the two main constituents of virtually all later Romantic interpretations of the Ninth Symphony: the idea that it depicts Beethoven's own quest for joy, and the idea that it represents a new synthesis of instrumental and vocal music. It was left to Wagner to draw these two ideas together, and so to create the definitive Romantic interpretation of the Ninth Symphony.

Wagner's Ninth

Wagner's commentaries on the Ninth Symphony span the thirty-year period from 1840, when he wrote a short story called 'A pilgrimage to Beethoven', to 1870, when he published an essay (simply called 'Beethoven') to mark the centenary of the composer's birth. These commentaries reflect the development of Wagner's thinking as a whole, and in particular his evolving conception of the music drama. Or maybe we should put it the other way round, and say that Wagner's thinking about the music drama reflects his evolving conception of the Ninth Symphony.

The universal Ninth

'A pilgrimage to Beethoven' reflects the rekindling of Wagner's enthusiasm for the Ninth Symphony as a result of hearing it played under Habeneck. It tells the story of a poor young German musician who is obsessed by Beethoven and sets out on a pilgrimage to Vienna, hoping to catch a glimpse of the great composer. After the vicissitudes demanded by the literary genre, the young composer obtains an audience with Beethoven, who tells him about his newest project, a symphony with choruses. It seems as if Beethoven has been reading Marx's 1826 review, for he talks about the synthesis of instrumental and vocal music in very much the same way that Marx did:

The instruments represent the rudimentary organs of Creation and Nature; what they express can never be clearly defined or put into words, for they reproduce the primitive feelings themselves, those feelings which issued from the chaos of the first Creation, when maybe there was not as yet one human being to take them up into his heart. 'Tis quite otherwise with the genius of the human voice; that represents the heart of man and its sharp-cut individual emotion. Its character is consequently restricted, but definite and clear. Now, let us bring these two elements together, and unite them![17]

Wagner's (or rather Wagner's Beethoven's) idea of vocal music having a clarity that instrumental music lacks already goes beyond Marx. And the idea that the Ninth Symphony represents some kind of creation myth – an idea that many later writers took up – not only adds definition to Marx's contrast between human and non-human, but universalizes the message of the work.

For the performance of the Ninth Symphony in Dresden six years later, Wagner wrote a lengthy programme note which was distributed to the audience. It consisted of a movement-by-movement commentary, with the first three movements being illustrated by quotations from Goethe's *Faust*. 'With the opening of the last movement', Wagner writes,

Beethoven's music takes on a more definitely *speaking* character: it quits the mould of purely instrumental music, observed in all the three preceding movements, the mode of infinite, indefinite expression; the musical poem is urging toward a crisis, a crisis only to be voiced in human speech. . . . A human voice, with the clear, sure utterance of articulate words, confronts the din of instruments. . . . With these words Light breaks on Chaos; a sure and definite mode of utterance is won, in which, supported by the conquered element of instrumental music, we now may hear expressed with clearness what boon it is the agonizing quest of Joy shall find as highest, lasting happiness.[18]

The basic framework of Wagner's interpretation is still the same as Marx's. Wagner's reference to the conquered element of instrumental music echoes Marx's description of the instruments subordinating themselves to the voice. But what Marx offers as a philosophical commentary becomes a dramatic scenario in Wagner's hands: the entry of the baritone soloist becomes the resolution of a crisis. And Wagner's earlier idea of the Ninth Symphony representing some kind of creation myth gains a biblical resonance when Wagner speaks of light breaking on chaos, so aligning the symphony with the book of Genesis.

Wagner also draws upon Fröhlich, or at any rate upon the kind of autobiographical interpretation of the Ninth Symphony that Fröhlich offered. Before the performance, Wagner published three anonymous notices about the Ninth Symphony in the *Dresdener Anzeiger*; they were part of the publicity campaign I mentioned in chapter 3.[19] In one of them, Wagner characterizes the symphony as Beethoven's attempt to reach out from the solitude of his deafness: 'When you meet the poor man, who cries to you so longingly,' asks Wagner, 'will you pass him on the other side if you find you do not understand his speech at once?' (The reader is evidently cast in the role of the Good Samaritan.) In the programme note itself, however, Wagner moves beyond a purely autobiographical interpretation. Like Fröhlich, he sees the first movement as representing a struggle, and the two middle movements as representing different aspects of joy. But the struggle and joy are not Beethoven's alone. Again Wagner universalizes the message. In the first movement, he draws a picture of epic combat:

'We think we see two giant wrestlers: each of whom desists once more, invincible. In passing gleams of light we recognize the sad-sweet smile of a happiness that seems to seek for us, for whose possession we strive, but whose attainment that arch-fiend withholds, overshadowing us with its pitch-black wings; so even our distant glimpse of bliss is troubled, and back we sink to gloomy brooding. . . . At the movement's close this gloomy, joyless mood, expanding to colossal form, appears to span the All, in awful majesty to take possession of a world that God had made for – *Joy*.

The emotional tone of this commentary is quite close to Kanne's or Fröhlich's. But there is an important rhetorical difference. Kanne describes what *Beethoven* does: he places obstacles in the path of his upward-rushing stream of fire, he forces his phrases down into the depths. In Wagner's account, by contrast, the operative pronoun is a confidential 'we': *we* strive for possession, *we* sink back to gloomy brooding. And if in the first movement Wagner casts the listener in the role of a more or less passive spectator, his account of the subsequent movements stresses active participation. 'With the very first rhythms of [the] second movement', writes Wagner, 'a wild excitement seizes us: a new world we enter, wherein we are swept on to frenzied orgy.' The trio represents a 'scene of earthly jollity'; but, says Wagner,

we are not disposed to view this banal gaiety as the goal of our restless quest of happiness and noble joy; our gaze clouds over, and we turn from the scene to trust ourselves anew to that untiring force which spurs us on without a pause to light upon that bliss which, ah! we never *thus* shall light on; for once again, at the movement's close, we are driven to that earlier scene of jollity, and now we thrust it with impatience from us so soon as recognized.

Like Fröhlich, Wagner interprets the music as a quest for joy, and comments on a technical feature (the brief return of the Trio at the end of the movement) when it contributes to the emotional expression of the music; but Wagner adds to this an element of moral choice, actively involving the listener in the making of that choice. And this participatory element reaches a climax in the finale. 'In the transport of Joy', writes Wagner,

a vow of *Universal Brotherhood* leaps from the overflowing breast; uplifted in spirit, we turn from embracing the whole human race to the great Creator of Nature, whose beatific Being we consciously attest. . . . It is as if a revelation had confirmed us in the blest belief that *every human soul is made for Joy*.

The social aspect that Wagner stresses – Georges Pioch would later refer to the Ninth Symphony as 'the great social act of music'[20] – is already implicit in the text of 'An die Freude'. The very form of Schiller's poem, consisting as it does of stanzas with intervening choruses, is social. And one of the stanzas that Beethoven did not set consists of an oath which the poet swears with his friends: they pledge themselves to courage, sympathy, and the pursuit of truth.

The revolutionary Ninth

In Wagner's 1846 programme, these ideas are not given a political interpretation. But they soon acquired one. The revolutionary fervour that swept through Europe during 1848 reached Dresden the following year. The city was already in a state of ferment when Wagner gave his third, and final, performance of the Ninth Symphony there, on 1 April. In *My Life*, Wagner says that one of the revolutionary leaders, Michael Bakunin, came to the concert; at the end of it he called out to Wagner that 'if all music were to be lost in the coming world conflagration, we should risk our own lives to preserve this symphony.' A month later there were troops in the streets, and on 7 May the opera house where Wagner had given the performance went up in flames; one of the guards at the barricades called out to Wagner, 'Herr Kapellmeister, the spark of divine joy [*Freude schöner Götterfunken*] has certainly ignited everything, the rotten building has burnt to the ground.' Coming so unexpectedly, says Wagner, 'this dramatic cry had a curiously strengthening and liberating effect on me'. Wagner thoroughly identified himself with the revolutionary cause, and when the revolution collapsed he had to leave Dresden in a hurry; he fled first to Weimar, and then via Zürich to Paris. During the whole of the journey, Wagner says, he fancied that he could hear the 'Joy' melody in the sound of the carriage wheels as they turned.[21]

Wagner's repeated references to the Ninth Symphony in this political context are not fortuitous. During April – between the performance and his flight from Dresden – he wrote a short article, which he never published, called 'The Revolution'.[22] This article is full of echoes of the Ninth Symphony programme of three years earlier. It begins with essentially the same scenario. In place of the two giant wrestlers of the symphony programme, the 1849 article depicts 'the lofty goddess Revolution'; she 'comes rustling on the wings of storm, her stately head ringed round with lightnings, a sword in her right hand, a torch in her left'. And where the first movement of the symphony offered a vision of happiness to its listeners, only to cast them down into a state of gloomy brooding, the 1849 article paints a picture of 'the hundred-thousands, millions', who are 'camped upon the hills and gaze into the distance, where thickening clouds proclaim the advent of emancipating Revolution; they all, . . who have *never* known joy, encamp there on the heights and strain their eyes in blissful expectation of her coming, and listen in rapt silence to the rustle of the rising storm'.

If the millions of this vision, and their quest for joy, echo the words of 'An die Freude', the reference becomes unmistakable a few pages later: 'Nor hate, nor envy, grudge, nor enmity, be henceforth found among you; as *brothers* shall ye all who live know one another, and *free*, free in willing, *free* in doing, *free* in enjoying.' Just as, in the second stanza of his poem, Schiller draws a division between those who will follow the path of joy and those who dare not, so Wagner's goddess proclaims: '*Two* peoples, only, are there from henceforth: the one, that follows me, the other that withstands me. The one I lead to happiness; over the other grinds my path.' (Again the biblical reference can hardly be missed.) And as the goddess finishes her address, 'the legions on the hill . . . fall to their knees and listen in mute transport'; *Ihr stürzt nieder, Millionen?*

But it is not just the resonances between Schiller's words and Wagner's article that reveal the influence of the Ninth Symphony on Wagner's thinking at this time. The millions of 'The Revolution' change from passive spectators to active participants in just the same way as their counterparts from the 1846 programme. 'In godlike ecstasy they leap from the ground,' Wagner concludes;

the poor, the hungering, the bowed by misery, are they no longer; proudly they raise themselves erect, inspiration shines from their ennobled faces, a radiant light streams from their eyes, and with the heaven-shaking cry *I am a Man!* the millions, the embodied Revolution, the God become Man, rush down to the valleys and plains, and proclaim to all the world the new gospel of Happiness.

To see how Wagner's political message is rooted in his interpretation of the Ninth Symphony, we need only compare this with the final words of the 1846 programme: 'We clasp the whole world to our breast; shouts and laughter fill the air, like thunder from the clouds, the roaring of the sea; whose everlasting tides and healing shocks lend life to earth, and keep life sweet, for the *joy* of Man to whom God gave the earth as home of *happiness*.'

It was during the year and a half after his flight from Dresden that Wagner developed the theory of the music drama. The first of the major writings devoted to this, *The Artwork of the Future*, dates from the autumn of 1849, and political and aesthetic thinking are inextricably intertwined in it. The Ninth Symphony again appears at a critical juncture. Wagner is pursuing a rather extravagant allegory in which Beethoven, in the guise of a mariner, sets out from the old world of instrumental music to discover the new world. Land is in sight.

Staunchly he threw his anchor out; and this anchor was *the Word* . . . '*Freude!*' With this word he cries to men: '*Breast to breast, ye mortal millions! This one kiss to all the world!*' – And *this Word* will be the language of the *Art-work of the Future*. – The Last Symphony of Beethoven is the redemption of Music from out her own peculiar element into the realm of *universal Art*. It is the human Evangel of the art of the Future. Beyond it no forward step is possible; for upon it the perfect Art-work of the Future alone can follow, the *universal Drama* to which Beethoven has forged for us the key.[23]

The tone of this passage is not unlike that of 'The Revolution'; there is the same gathering crisis and quest for a solution. But the solution that Wagner offers is now aesthetic rather than political; the goddess Revolution has turned into the Evangel of the art of the Future. Beethoven's last symphony has become the first music drama. Not surprisingly, Wagner has been roundly accused of appropriating the Ninth Symphony to his own ends in this passage. We can hardly deny the charge. But we could rephrase it, by saying that the music drama was already implicit in Wagner's interpretation of the Ninth Symphony as a social and dramatic event. Seen this way, the Ninth Symphony becomes a principal focus of Wagner's evolving conception of the music drama. And if it largely drops out of Wagner's writings over the next twenty years, that is perhaps because it was, in effect, absorbed into the succession of music dramas that occupied him during that period.

As I said, Wagner's last extended discussion of the Ninth Symphony dates from 1870, when he published his centenary essay 'Beethoven'. As in 1849, he speaks of Beethoven leaving the confines of instrumental music behind him; like the seafaring Beethoven of 1849, the Beethoven of 1870 'set foot on that new world of Light' which is embodied in the music drama.[24] And again it is the first entry of the voice around which Wagner's thoughts revolve. But the tone has changed since 1849. 'It is not the meaning of the Word', says Wagner,

that really takes us with this entry of the human voice, but the human character of that voice. Neither is it the thought expressed in Schiller's verses, that occupies our minds thereafter, but the familiar sound of the choral chant; in which we feel ourselves bidden to join and thus take part in an ideal Divine Service, as the congregation really did at entry of the Chorale in S. Bach's great Passions. In fact it is obvious, especially with the chief-melody proper, that Schiller's words have been built in perforce and with no great skill; for this melody had first unrolled its breadth before us as an entity *per se*, entrusted to the instruments alone, and there had thrilled us with the nameless joy of a paradise regained. . . . It then becomes the *cantus firmus*, the Chorale of the new communion.

It is curious to find Marx's rather tortuous argument about the deficient setting of the text resurfacing after a lapse of forty-four years. But more significant is the manner in which the social aspect of the Ninth Symphony has been transformed from drama to something nearer ritual. Two years later, during the preparations for the Bayreuth performance of the symphony, Wagner reiterated his remarks about the congregation joining in. In a letter dated 7 April 1872 he wrote that 'The chief thing is an inspiring *Musical Festival*; the chorus of the symphony should really be sung by the entire audience.'[25] As ever, the Ninth Symphony provides a window into Wagner's mind. The religious elements in Wagner's interpretation of the work (to which I have already drawn attention) are coming to the fore. The concert hall is turning into a *Bühnenfestspielhaus*. Beethoven's last symphony is no longer the first music drama; it has become the precursor of *Parsifal*.

In 1877, Ludwig Nohl published an account of the Ninth Symphony in which he claimed that the finale 'represents the solution of the conflicts of this tragedy of life'.[26] The chorus, he says, 'sings of joy as the transfiguration of the earthly world by eternal love. The will can accomplish nothing greater than to sacrifice itself for the good of the whole.' And he adds: 'Is it claiming too much to say that out of the spirit of this music a "new civilization" and an existence more worthy of human beings might be developed, since it leads us back to the foundation and source of civilization and human existence – to religion?' Pervaded as it is by the influence of Schopenhauer, Nohl's commentary seems to have little or nothing to do with Beethoven. But it has everything to do with the political and religious meanings that Wagner found in the Ninth Symphony and embodied in his own artistic work. One might think that Nohl was talking about Wagner's Ninth Symphony, not Beethoven's. And of course, he was.

Fig. 1 Waldmüller's portrait of Beethoven (1823)

Wagner's Beethoven, or the importance of being earnest

On 5 March 1869 Wagner wrote Hermann Härtel, of the publishing firm
Breitkopf and Härtel, to ask if he could have a copy made of Ferdinand
Waldmüller's portrait of Beethoven, which was owned by the publishing firm
(Fig. 1).[27] Härtel gave his assent, but pointed out that Waldmüller's portrait,
which dates from 1823, had been painted in a hurry and heavily criticized by
Beethoven's contemporaries. This was quite true; Schindler launched a
vitriolic attack on it, explaining that Beethoven had been unwilling to sit for
it and that, as a result, Waldmüller had had to work largely from memory.
'The Waldmüller portrait', wrote Schindler, 'is, if possible, further from the
truth than any other. . . . It has nothing in common with the head of
Beethoven, the composer in whose mind there was evolving at that time the
ninth symphony.'[28] Schindler, however, does nothing to strengthen his case
by citing Rochlitz's account of how Beethoven looked at their non-existent
meeting at Baden in 1822,[29] and then proceeding to judge the value of different
portraits of Beethoven according to how well they correspond with Rochlitz's

Fig. 2 Krausse's copy of the Waldmüller portrait

description! And we should bear in mind that Waldmüller was then, and remains now, one of the most highly respected painters of his generation.

Wagner wrote back to Härtel, saying that the fact that the painting had been done in a hurry was what made it the most realistic and unaffected of all the Beethoven portraits, and that he wanted exactly those qualities preserved in the copy. He said the same to Robert Krausse, who made the copy, and afterwards complimented him on the fidelity of his work: 'With this artistically executed copy I possess everything that I had wished to possess: an unaffected, real portrait of Beethoven.' Krausse had worked fast; the portrait was installed in Villa Wahnfried, Wagner's Bayreuth residence, on 1 July 1869. It is reproduced as Fig. 2. Is it as accurate a copy as Wagner made it out to be? Not according to the art historian, Alessandra Comini. She writes:

The eyeglasses of Biedermeier objectivity through which Waldmüller had viewed and painted his unidealized model have been exchanged for the subjective spectacles of Romanticism, with which both Krausse and Wagner unconsciously saw their Beethoven. What had originally attracted Wagner to this – the least beloved by commercial mythographers – image of Beethoven was the very fact that it showed Beethoven the aging man, not Beethoven the perpetually youthful hero. But the titanic aspect of that man – his silver-streaked hair, his incipient frown, his compressed lips, have all been, almost involuntarily, enhanced. Krausse clarified, as it were, the impress of suffering and mighty mental activity.[30]

In Krausse's copy of the Waldmüller portrait we see the composer of Wagner's Ninth Symphony. We see the unremittingly earnest Beethoven of whom Wagner wrote that 'His moral principles were of the strictest bourgeois stripe; a frivolous tone would make him foam. . . . We see a . . . force at work in him to vehemently ward off a frivolous tendency of life and mind.'[31] In fact Wagner may well have had Krausse's copy before his very eyes as he wrote these words; they come from the centenary essay, which appeared rather over a year after Wagner took delivery of the painting.

5

The twentieth-century Ninth

The purely musical Ninth

In *Opera and Drama*, which was written in 1850–51, Wagner pursues an involved argument about the nature of melody. He contrasts the organic nature of folksong with the mechanical complication of the operatic aria. He argues that true melody is shaped from union with words, and not according to the arbitrary patterns of so-called musical form. And he suggests that, in the Ninth Symphony, Beethoven actually embodies this process of melodic shaping in the music. He is referring, of course, to the 'Joy' theme.

Though *only in the progress* of his tone-piece, does the master set his full melody before us as a finished whole, yet this melody is to be subsumed as already finished in the artist's mind *from the beginning*. He merely broke at the outset the narrow Form, . . . he shattered it into its component parts, in order to unite them by organic creation into a new whole; and this he did, by setting the component parts of different melodies in changeful contact with each other, as though to show the organic affinity of the seemingly most diverse of such parts, and therewith the prime affinity of those different melodies themselves.

Wagner is saying that the relationship of its various melodic materials to the 'Joy' theme gives the Ninth Symphony an underlying coherence – a real form beneath the surface form, so to speak. At least, this is what Alexander Serov, Wagner's Russian disciple, understood him to be saying. And in his own writings, Serov developed this idea a good deal further. The whole of the Ninth Symphony, he says, is unified by a 'great monothematic plan'. Serov means this in both a programmatic and a technical sense. The theme of the symphony, he says, is the idea of brotherhood, the musical expression of which is the 'Joy' theme. While this theme appears in explicit form in the last movement, it is implied in all that precedes it. Serov gives specific instances of the anticipation of the 'Joy' theme in earlier movements. He refers, for instance, to the melody in the woodwinds at bar 74 of the first movement, which rises from E♭ through F to G, and then down by step to C – just like the 'Joy' theme, apart from the different inflection of the E. And he finds equally clear anticipations of the 'Joy' theme in the second movement. From all this, Serov concludes that the basic principle underlying the Ninth Symphony is the 'transformation of a *single* idea through a "chain of metamorphoses"'.[1]

Serov wrote in Russian and, though his ideas were mentioned by Wilhelm von Lenz and Grove, they had little influence on his contemporaries. But they form the starting point of an important twentieth-century story. Just a hundred years after *Opera and Drama* came out, the pianist and critic Rudolph Réti published a book called *The Thematic Process in Music*, in which he gave a much more detailed technical interpretation to the ideas that Serov had put forward.[2] Réti intended his analytical approach to be applicable to all the masterworks of the classical tradition; but once again it is the Ninth Symphony that is invoked as the star witness.

Réti divides the various thematic materials of the symphony into a number of motives, generally of three or four notes, and shows how the same motives can be found in all the different themes – if not in the same form or transposed, then upside down, or backwards. He shows how there are particular affinities between the first subjects of all four movements, and again between their second subjects. He also calls attention to the relationship between D to B♭ that permeates the symphony: melodically, in the first subject of the opening movement (bars 21–4); harmonically, in the first chord of the finale (which he sees as a superimposition of the B♭ major and D minor triads); and structurally, in the key relations within the first and last movements, as well as the relationship of the third movement to the others. On the basis of all this, Réti concludes that the Ninth Symphony embodies 'the most manifold, most effective, and most logical architectural interconnections'; in fact he comes close to quoting Serov when he says that 'in a wider sense . . . one thematic idea permeates the whole work'.[3]

Réti's analytical approach has been widely criticized and I am not going to repeat the arguments here; the basic problem is that if you chop up the music into small enough pieces, and pick out just those notes that fit the theory, you are bound to find the same patterns reduplicated everywhere.[4] What is more relevant, in view of the considerable influence that Réti's ideas had in the 1950s and 60s, is to ask what motivates them. In part, Réti's analysis is a vindication of the coherence of the Ninth Symphony; this becomes obvious when he writes that 'Even Beethoven's Ninth Symphony, that pinnacle of structural consistency and perfection, was not safe from the absurd insinuation that its architecture is not truly organic. . . . Such intimations are pure nonsense.'[5]

But this is really incidental to his main aim, which is to show that the Ninth Symphony is coherent *in purely musical terms*. Réti is using a technique deriving ultimately from Wagner in order to demonstrate that Wagner's own style of programmatic interpretation is misguided and redundant. The music, says Réti, can stand on its own.

The absolute music polemic

Réti joined the game rather late. The basic purpose of Schenker's monograph on the Ninth Symphony, which was published nearly forty years before Réti's book, is to refute the whole edifice of Wagnerian interpretation, and to reclaim the work for what Schenker calls 'absolute music'. This term has always been polemical. It was coined by Wagner; in fact it first appears in the programme note for the 1846 performance of the Ninth Symphony, where Wagner describes the instrumental recitative as 'almost breaking the bounds of absolute music'.[6] For Wagner the term had, or at any rate soon acquired, a negative connotation: absolute music stood for the old world of instrumental music that he had left behind. But the term was taken up, now in a positive sense, by those who opposed Wagner's demotion of the symphony to the pre-history of the music drama. Schenker's attempt to show how everything in the Ninth Symphony, even its finale, can be explained in purely musical terms is therefore an accurately targeted assault on the central stronghold of the Wagnerian aesthetic.

In the Preface of his monograph, Schenker makes an astonishing assertion: 'In the beginning was content!'[7] By 'content' (*Inhalt*) Schenker means purely musical content; he is rewriting the opening of St John's Gospel in the spirit of absolute music. (What makes this strategy puzzling is that the Bible seems to be on Wagner's side.) Schenker explains what he means. A proper analysis of the content of the Ninth Symphony, he says, makes it possible to 'specify the tonal necessities, hidden until now, that caused it to arise in exactly one way and not in any other'.[8] The nub of his claim, then, is that the Ninth Symphony (like all musical masterworks) can be explained in exclusively musical terms, leaving no remainder for which extra-musical explanations have to be invoked. Wagner and his acolytes put forward their literary interpretations of Beethoven's music because they lacked the ability to grasp it musically. Instead of clarifying anything at all, they created such a fog of verbiage that they altogether lost sight of the true nature of Beethoven's music. It is Schenker's self-appointed task to lay bare the image of the Ninth Symphony as it really is.

The fall guy of Schenker's monograph is Hermann Kretzschmar, who published a series of repertory guides for music-lovers in the late 1880s under the title *Führer durch den Konzert-Saal*. These guides avoided technicalities, and for Schenker (who despised music-lovers) they typified the worst kind of post-Wagnerian verbosity. From Schenker's remarks one might conclude that Kretzschmar was musically illiterate; in fact he was a conductor and a musicologist of some distinction. In an article addressed to specialists rather than the general public, Kretzschmar set out a rationale for 'musical hermeneutics', as he called his style of interpretation. He bases this rationale on the emotions or 'affections' that music expresses. 'It is the task of hermeneutics', he says, 'to distil these "affections" from the music and to describe in words the basic pattern of their development.'[9] What he is outlining here is essentially the same kind of interpretation as Kanne and Fröhlich offered: the construction of a literary analogue to the music.

To a considerable extent, Kretzschmar's aims actually coincided with Schenker's. The purpose of hermeneutics, says Kretzschmar, is 'to identify the irreducible core of thought in every sentence of a writer and in every detail of an artist's work; to explain and analyse the whole by obtaining the clearest possible understanding of every smallest detail – and all this by employing every aid that technical knowledge, general culture, and personal talent can supply'. It was certainly Schenker's aim, as much as Kretzschmar's, to explain the mutual relationship between part and whole in music. The essential difference is a negative one: Schenker insists that this can, and should, be done purely in terms of 'technical knowledge', without any reference to 'general culture' or 'personal talent'. And that is what he tries to do in the Ninth Symphony monograph.

As might be expected, it is when Schenker deals with the finale that the polemical motivation of his analysis becomes most obvious. Wagner's extra-musical explanation of the opening of the finale (or Kretzschmar's, which follows similar lines) can only be refuted by an analysis that explains the entire plan in terms of purely musical organization. Schenker pulls no punches. This is how he begins his discussion:

The instinct for purely musical laws did not desert Beethoven even when he wrote 'program' music or vocal music. An offense against musical logic – logic in the absolute sense, understood as completely separate from program or text – was by nature simply impossible for him; and so in this case too, as he set about composition of the Schiller text, he again let himself be guided – in spite of text – only by laws of absolute musical organization.[10]

Schenker explains that Beethoven's intention at the beginning of the finale is, as everyone knows, to create the effect of searching for a new theme. Strictly speaking, he says, this programme is incapable of realization: 'the suitability of a theme in music can never be established in advance of its development', and its developmental potential obviously cannot be tested in this manner.[11] Again, while Beethoven's programmatic intentions dictated the entry of voices into a symphonic work, 'It did not occur to him that perhaps no justification in the world could be sufficient to motivate adequately the sudden clash of two elements so different by nature!' There is, in other words, an irrevocable contradiction between the demands of the programme and of absolute music.

Wagner, of course, would have agreed with the last point; that is why, for Wagner, the Ninth Symphony spelled the end of absolute music. But Schenker turns the argument around. Beethoven, he says, was keenly aware of this contradiction. Being Beethoven, he didn't abandon the plan just because it was impossible; instead, he took care to carry it out in such a way that the demands of absolute music were met as far as they possibly could be. In order to substantiate this, Schenker explains the entire section of the finale up to bar 594 as a massively enlarged antecedent-consequent structure. This, he says, accounts for the repetition of the opening fanfare (bars 1, 208) and the passages of recitative that follow; it explains why the rest of each subsection consists of variations on the 'Joy' theme. But the second subsection (bars 208–594) shouldn't be seen as simply a repetition of the first, only with the voices added, along the lines of a concerto exposition;[12] there is a continuous process of dynamic intensification throughout the entire section. In this way, Schenker concludes, there is a parallelism between the two subsections, but the first leads to the second; that is what it means to call them antecedent and consequent. And this, of course, is a purely musical relationship.

Schenker is clearly conscious of the special pleading in this argument. He tries to anticipate objections:

The inner relation of the two parts under consideration [he is referring to bars 1–207 and 208–594] is so strong that the difference in quantity and type of variations does not at all come significantly into consideration as a counterforce. Against the fact that the two parts present nothing but variations on the same theme, what can it signify that the first part, scored purely instrumentally, shows three variations (apart from the recitatives and the theme itself), while the second, vocal, part shows as many as five such (again ignoring the recitative)? And if, moreover, in the first part all variations are in D major and follow directly upon one another, while in the second part one of the variations (the fourth) is in B♭ major, and at the same point the direct succession is broken – what is the importance of all this in comparison to the commonness of thrust of the two parts?[13]

It is all too easy to imagine what Schenker (who trained as a lawyer) would have made of all these imbalances and exceptions had he been on the other side of the controversy. And in a real lawyer's argument, he manages to turn the entry of the voices, which he had described as incompatible with absolute music, into the crowning demonstration of his case. If Beethoven was to bring in the voices, Schenker says, then the least he could do was to prepare their entry by having the instruments play the theme before it was sung:

> For if the vocal strain presents a thematic material that is already known to us from what precedes it, there is at least in this thematic relationship a halfway acceptable, independent, and also – note well – musically absolute justification for its appearance! It is, then, the consequent-like quality, so to speak, in its construction – what a great triumph of the absolute-musical law! – which is able to make a fundamentally unfulfillable assignment possible up to a certain point! Precisely this route of an antecedent-consequent construction is the one that Beethoven has actually taken![14]

The case rests.

The return of the horror fanfare

If there is one moment in the Ninth Symphony that acts as a litmus test for different interpretations of the work, it is bar 208 of the final movement, when the *Schreckensfanfare* returns with renewed force.

Kretzschmar, Schenker's *bête noire*, offers his usual kind of descriptive commentary. He begins a few bars before the return of the horror fanfare. The music 'goes reeling back,' he writes, 'after a moment of uncertain thrashing-about, to that terrible scene with which the movement began. Help again arrives. This time it is the singer of the baritone solo who restores order with the words inserted by Beethoven himself: "O Freunde, nicht diese Töne . . .".' Schenker quotes this passage but can barely restrain himself:

> How inadvertently comical that the commentator . . . speaks of the bold transition and coda as a 'moment of uncertain thrashing about'; how naive that he construes, obviously in trying to help himself out of a shameful embarrassment, nothing other than embarrassment on Beethoven's part: 'Help again arrives' – by which, however, he intends nothing more nor less than to do away with the musically organic necessity of the second part![15]

The gap between Schenker and Kretzschmar is unbridgeable. Schenker's objection is not simply that Kretzschmar is wrong. It is that Kretzschmar creates a literary analogue for the music, instead of explaining it in musical terms; in short, that he tries to interpret in a non-technical manner. Schenker puts the difference between himself and Kretzschmar in a nutshell when he remarks, a few lines later, 'I am more interested in the compositional function of, for example, an eighth note rest . . . than in all of Kretzschmar's interpretations.'

Like Kretzschmar, Martin Cooper discusses the passage in non-technical terms. But he adopts a more critical standpoint. The quotations from the earlier movements have already worried him: 'the situation is a little too like a musical quiz or conundrum for the beginning of a great symphonic movement,' he says.[16] And he continues:

It is certainly not improved when the *Schreckensfanfare* and the recitatives (this time with words attached) reappear long after the listener has received the impression of being well advanced into the movement. . . . Musicians and music-lovers have mostly come to accept this unsatisfactory opening to the finale not simply because it represents a comparatively small blot on a very great work, but because that very blot is so completely characteristic of the composer.

Vaughan Williams takes this common-sense approach a stage further (or could he be satirizing it?) when he writes that 'If we knew only the printed page and knew nothing of the historical facts, we might well guess that Beethoven originally designed a purely instrumental Finale on "sonata" lines, that he changed his mind and decided instead on a choral conclusion, but that he forgot when he sent the work to the printers to cut out the discarded version.'[17]

For the critic in the *Edinburgh Review*, on the other hand, the passage is fundamentally misconceived. 'This employment of music', he writes, 'involves a perfectly false aesthetic. It is the employment of sounds that are literally and materially harsh, instead of the symbolizing of harshness by the legitimate use of musical expression.'[18] Like most of this critic's views, this is a throwback to eighteenth-century thinking; Mozart would have agreed with him. Even Berlioz, who combined ultra-romanticism with a strongly classicizing tendency, reserved his judgement as to whether or not the fanfare was 'an infringement on the dignity of art'. But this was not Berlioz's main concern. He was mystified as to what Beethoven meant by either this or the preceding fanfare. 'I see a formal intention,' he writes, 'a calculated and thought-out project, producing two chords at the two instants preceding the successive appearances of vocal and instrumental recitative. Although I have searched high and low for the reason behind this idea, I am forced to admit that it is unknown to me.'[19]

It's a pity that Berlioz was not sitting next to Schumann's Florestan, whose neighbour quaked when he heard the first horror fanfare; Florestan turned to him and asked, 'What else is this chord, dear cantor, but a common chord with an anticipatory dominant note in a somewhat complicated distribution (because one is uncertain whether to take the A of the timpani or the F of the bassoon for the bass)?'[20] But according to Réti, Florestan got it wrong. As I said, Réti explains the first fanfare as a superimposition of the B♭ major and D minor triads; it compresses the principal key relationship of the symphony into a single harmony. As for the second fanfare, it consists of all of the notes of the D minor scale – 'the very notes from which the Allegro's main theme . . . is formed, which is in turn the source for all the themes of the symphony'. In this way, says Réti, Beethoven 'attempted to force, as it were, the entire thematic content into one chord'. He admits that Beethoven embarked on this course by virtue of a programmatic vision. 'But', he continues, 'this vision was materialized through musical, that is structural and, in particular, thematic means.'[21] Absolute music is vindicated once again. It always is in Réti.

One might expect to find Schenker adopting the same kind of position as Réti in regard to this passage. But he does not. Instead, he approaches it from a common-sense angle rather similar to Cooper's:

Just consider: after a long struggle the composer finally settles on his theme, which he immediately celebrates in several variations; is the chosen theme now supposed still not to have been the correct one, and the quest for a new theme to begin once again from the outset? What does it mean, then, when Beethoven proclaims: 'Friends, not these tones! Let more pleasant ones inspire us instead, and more joyful!' (as in the words of the recitative read in the consequent, bars 217–236), after he has just found and bid welcome to the 'more pleasant and joyful' one? Let nobody object that Beethoven's words 'not these tones' might perhaps have related only to the recent chaotic, stormy outbreak of bars 209–215; for the figuration of the D-minor triad by itself no more expresses any kind of 'tone' here than it did earlier in the first Part, since by actual 'tones' Beethoven could have understood only more or less clearly forged 'themes' as the bearers of particular emotional states.[22]

What begins as a common-sense argument thus ends up as something very different. Schenker creates the problem for himself by insisting that when Beethoven writes 'not these tones' he must be referring to specific themes.

Why does Schenker do this? The reason is that he is determined at all costs not to accept Wagner's interpretation of the passage. I have already quoted from the description of it in Wagner's 1846 programme:

Once again, yet louder than before, the wild chaotic yell of unslaked passion storms our ear. Then a human voice, with the clear, sure utterance of articulate words, confronts the din of instruments; and we know not at which to wonder most, the boldness of the inspiration, or the naivety of the master who lets that voice address the instruments as follows: 'Friends, not these tones'![23]

In Wagner's interpretation, then, 'not these tones' refers to the horror fanfare, to the first three movements, ultimately to instrumental music as a whole. Virtually all commentators accept this line of interpretation. In fact it is hard to see what Beethoven could have done to make his meaning plainer; the passage fully justifies Joseph Kerman's description of the aging composer 'battering at the communications barrier with every weapon of his knowledge'.[24]

Schenker insists on misinterpreting Beethoven because he will not admit the possibility of a purely extra-musical logic. In fact he turns the very illogicality of the passage, as he reads it, into yet another vindication of absolute music:

> At the beginning of the consequent section we thus face a logical inconsistency, which fortunately finds its remedy once again in Beethoven's musically absolute primal urge towards parallelism! How much light now falls on the power of Beethoven's invincible, purely musical instincts from precisely such an inconsistency! From the standpoint of the world of tones, he perceived the simple necessity of a repetition of the head of the antecedent as so strong that he was able to overlook the infraction from the programmatic standpoint! How can anybody, in the face of such a blatant fact, still support the myth of Beethoven's abdication of instrumental music in favor of vocal as the only justifiable category?[25]

The logic of Schenker's argument is undeniable, but it is a looking-glass logic. It is disturbing to see one of the great musicians of the twentieth century so consumed by a polemical intention that he has lost the ability to respond in a direct, uncomplicated manner to what Beethoven wrote.

Domesticating the Ninth

Like Cooper, Schenker is worried by the quotations from previous movements in the finale.

> How could Beethoven, assuming he had in mind the selection of a new theme, seriously have arrived at the idea of testing the suitability of exactly the themes already used up by an earlier exposition – themes that could never again return(!) – instead of suggesting to the listener only new themes, one after another? The business of selecting one theme from several belongs under all circumstances only to the sketchbook.[26]

It is hard to know quite what to say about this. It is like trying to explain a joke. Schenker's insight fails when confronted with a passage that is not just music, but music about music – in Treitler's words, 'music interpreted by itself'.[27] The passages of recitative, together with the review of the themes from the first three movements, accomplish a kind of temporal modulation; the musical time of the first three movements is transformed into real time, the time of performance. To use terms which are unavoidably reminiscent of Wagner, musical time changes into dramatic or ritualistic time. Another way of putting this – which is no less reminiscent of Wagner – is that what began as a musical event turns at this point into a social one.

Music interpreted by itself

The commentary of the instrumental recitative on the themes from earlier movements, and the commentary of the baritone soloist on the horror fanfare, are the most overt instances of self-reference in the Ninth Symphony. But there are other respects in which the music is self-referential. Several times, Beethoven sets up a formal structure only to call it into question. This happens in the first movement. As I said in chapter 2, the development section represents a decrease in tension, which is contrary to normal classical practice. As Treitler expresses it, the final stages of the development are like 'genial busywork. But then quite suddenly at m. 301 the music stiffens. In retrospect most of the development seems suddenly like an unrealistic episode.'[28] One of the reasons for this is that, as Treitler says, the *fortissimo* D major passage 'simply asserts itself, not as a consequence of anything, not as a signal of what is to come'.[29] Yet this is the moment that, in a conventional sonata form, would be most unambiguously implied by what has come before, and that would most unambiguously point towards the final resolution. Beethoven has cast his movement in the mould of sonata form, but severed the links of implication and realization of which that form is an expression.

On the smaller scale, too, formal structures are repeatedly undermined by sentimental or rhetorical gestures. Grove describes one of these; his words seem to betray a curious sense of embarrassment.

Here I would call attention, though with reluctance, to a singular feature in this great work – namely, to the occurrence more than once during the working-out of the first movement of a vacillation or hesitancy of expression of which I know no trace in any of the other symphonies, but which cannot but be recognized here by a loyal hearer; where the notes of flutes and oboes seem to tremble and falter as if they were the utterance of human lips, the organs of an oppressed human heart. These places need not be specified, they cannot but strike the sympathetic listener, and almost suggest, if it be not disrespectful to entertain such a thought, that the great Beethoven was, with all his experience, too much overpowered by his feelings to find adequate expression for them.[30]

I assume that Grove is referring to the ritardando figure at bar 195, which recurs at bar 213 and then again at bars 506 and 510. These are, to be sure, just cadence figures. But they are so striking that they seem to cut across the structural sections in which they are embedded, giving rise to a rhetorical pattern that has little to do with sonata form. The effect is to create a kind of disjunction between form and expression.

And then there is the whole network of motivic links uncovered by Serov and Réti.[31] Most people assume, with Réti, that such links enhance the architectural unity of a work. But it makes at least as much sense to claim that they do the opposite; as Maynard Solomon puts it, they 'may in fact disrupt the organic flow of the materials and their orderly development'.[32] In the Ninth Symphony, these links seem to short-circuit the large-scale organization; the form, so to speak, collapses in upon itself. There are many other features of the music, particularly in the first movement, that add to this effect. There is the lack of strongly articulated cadential organization at phrase level which caused one contemporary critic to describe the movement as 'perhaps too restlessly active, without the necessary caesuras to organize the total impression'.[33] And there is the predominantly slow – sometimes very slow – harmonic rhythm, with changes of harmony frequently taking place across the barline; this, too, militates against the emergence of strongly articulated phrase structure.

Above all, there is the extraordinary diversity of thematic material. The basis of the classical style is the anonymous continuity material that sets themes, and thereby the form, into relief; but in the first movement of the Ninth Symphony everything seems to be thematic. As I said in chapter 2, the transitional material at bar 74 sounds almost as thematic as the main theme to which it leads, at bar 80; the result is that the beginning of the second group is not clearly projected as a point of formal arrival. And there are many such examples. Nineteenth-century critics commented on the resulting effect, though they did not describe it in these terms. In 1853, a Russian critic likened the movement to 'a gigantic tree, whose branches, reaching towards the earth, have taken root and formed a forest round their forebear'.[34] In the twentieth century, Friedrich Blume expressed the same idea less figuratively when he spoke, with reference to Beethoven's late music in general, of the unceasing series of motives that 'pour their energies directly into the movement'.[35] We can express this more technically by saying that the entire middleground level of thematic organization that typifies the classical style is, in effect, dropping out of the music. In this way, the first movement of the Ninth Symphony points towards the 'motivic web' of Wagner's music dramas.

From the largest scale to the level of moment-to-moment organization, then, the first movement of the Ninth Symphony is pervaded by internal tensions and disjunctions. But it is in the finale that the contradictions become flagrant. Time and again there are passages that are jarringly out of place in terms of tempo, tonality, style, or genre. One is the 'Gregorian fossil', as Cooper calls it,[36] of 'Brüder! über'm Sternenzelt' (bar 611). Then there is an entire network of Mozartean references, beginning with the tag appended to the 'Joy' theme at bar 267, which Cooper likens to the ritornello of Papageno's first aria in Act I, Scene 2 of *The Magic Flute*.[37] The next such reference is what Tovey calls the 'round-canon' in the coda (bar 783); 'nothing like it', he says, 'had been sounded in music since Mozart's *Magic Flute*', and again it is Papageno and Papagena that he has in mind.[38] Finally there is the unmistakably Mozartean choral cadence at bars 810–13, which is subsequently blown up into an astonishingly extravagant cadenza for the soloists at bars 832–42. This cadenza is at odds with its surroundings in terms of tempo, tonality, style, *and* genre; it is as if Beethoven has blundered into quite another piece.

But the most outrageously foreign element is the 'Turkish' music that begins at bar 331 with what the *Edinburgh Review* correspondent described as the 'absurd grunts for the contrafagotto'. The style is borrowed from the military music for wind and percussion instruments that eighteenth century European armies adopted from the Turkish Janissaries, and that regularly featured in military parades. 'That such sonorities,' says Cooper, 'with their military and popular associations, might well be suitable at the end of a big movement depicting communal rejoicing is plain; but to introduce them when the text speaks of the angelic host mustered around the throne of God and the music itself has fallen, as it were, into an "O altitudo!" seems almost perverse. That, however, is exactly what Beethoven does.'[39] And critics have spent the last hundred and seventy years trying to explain it. For Kanne, the Turkish music was just another element in the diversity of the finale.[40] For Fröhlich it symbolized the participation of all creatures in universal rejoicing, from the lowest orders of creation (represented by the bassoons and bass drum) up.[41] To Wagner it suggested 'a troop of striplings marching past', leading to a 'brilliant contest, expressed by instruments alone: we see the youths rush valiantly into the fight, whose victor's spoil is *Joy*'.[42] Each of these interpretations embodies the usual Romantic strategy: creating meaning out of incoherence.

The trouble with all such interpretations is that they domesticate what they explain. If we hear the diversity of nature in the 'Turkish' music, or see an army marching past, or if for that matter we view it as the second tonal area within a sonata-like structure, then we may succeed in not actually hearing the 'grunts' of the bassoons and bass drum at all – or at least, in not hearing them as 'absurd'. Romantic interpretations reduce the contradictory elements of the Ninth Symphony to a narrative thread or a series of pictures; absolute-music interpretations reduce them to an architectural plan. And the result in each case is the same: the music is deproblematized, sanitized, shrink-wrapped. As Michael Steinberg puts it, 'We have come to be awfully comfortable with Beethoven – comfortable, unshocked, and unshockable.'[43]

It takes a significant effort of mind to recapture the discomfiture of Fanny Mendelssohn, who heard her brother conduct the Ninth Symphony in 1836 and described it as 'a gigantic tragedy with a conclusion meant to be dithyrambic, but falling from its height into the opposite extreme – into burlesque'.[44] It is equally hard to understand the response of Gottfried Fink, who heard the symphony in 1826 and described the finale as

a festival of hatred towards all that can be called human joy. With gigantic strength the perilous hoard emerges, tearing hearts asunder and darkening the divine spark of the gods with noisy, monstrous mocking. . . . The master remains what he is, an exorcist, whom it has pleased this time to demand from us something superhuman. To this I do not consent.[45]

I do not think that the negative responses of these early listeners are by any means out of place. On the contrary, it seems to me that they have an essential contribution to make towards an adequate understanding of the Ninth Symphony.

The Ninth as ideology

The Ninth Symphony is full of what might be called 'unconsummated symbols' (with apologies to Susanne Langer). By this I mean such things as the 'funeral march' that begins at bar 513 of the first movement, the abrupt ending of the second movement, the military tones in the third movement, the climactic moves to the flat submediant in the third and fourth movements (bars 133 and 330 respectively), the Turkish music and the horror fanfares of the finale – all those elements that 'vibrate with an implied significance that overflows the musical scenario', as Solomon puts it.[46] And he continues: 'Beethoven . . . quite consciously wanted us to find "meaning" in the symphony's text, design, and tonal symbols.' We can hardly deny this. But we might enquire into the conditions for finding meaning in music. I would like to put forward three models of this – two now, and one in the Conclusion.

93

The first model of musical meaning is when a work has a predetermined message which either listeners grasp or they don't. Supermarket music either makes people buy more or it doesn't. Hearing the national anthem either inspires patriotic feelings or it doesn't. This model of musical meaning corresponds to what Wolfgang Iser, the literary critic, describes as pulp literature or propaganda.[47] As such terms imply, this is not a favoured model of the aesthetic process; perhaps the nearest example within the symphonic repertory is Richard Strauss's *Ein Heldenleben*. The principal model that Iser offers for the aesthetic process – the second model of musical meaning – is when the work embodies areas of indeterminacy; listeners, so to speak, insert their meanings into the gaps in the music, thereby creating their own interpretations of it. A good example of this is Schubert's *Winterreise*; the failure of this song cycle to specify elements that are essential for its interpretation explains why it is more powerful and more suggestive than Schubert's earlier cycle *Die schöne Müllerin*, which by comparison tends towards the first model of musical meaning.

To which of these models does the Ninth Symphony properly belong? There is certainly no lack of propagandist interpretations of it, and that in the narrowly political sense. Around the middle of the nineteenth century, Edgar Quinet described the finale of the Ninth Symphony as 'the Marseillaise of humanity', and asserted that the real subject of Schiller's 'An die Freude' is not Joy (*Freude*) at all, but Freedom (*Freiheit*).[48] This story, for which there was never any historical foundation, is one of the most abiding myths to have become attached to the Ninth Symphony. It seems to go back to a novel, *Das Musikfest*, which was published in 1838 by Wolfgang Griepenkerl. In this novel, one of the characters refers to the true meaning of Schiller's Ode, and an author's footnote reads: 'It was freedom.'[49] The idea that Schiller originally wrote an Ode to Freedom, but changed it to Joy for reasons of prudence or censorship, was popularized in France during the 1880s by Victor Wilder; and from there it got into Thayer's biography of Beethoven and Grove's book on the symphonies, so enjoying wide circulation.

The story has been repudiated on any number of occasions. Maurice Kufferath ridiculed it with reference to the second stanza of the Ode ('Whoever has taken a loving wife, let him join us in celebration!'); 'Applied to marriage,' he wrote, 'perhaps freedom means divorce? The *Ode to Joy*, a hymn to divorce. Ha! ha! Think about that. It's rich. A new idea, an altogether original interpretation.'[50]

But the idea of an 'Ode to Freedom' seems to be too deep-seated in a psychological or cultural sense for it to be amenable to refutation. In 1989, a special Christmas concert was held at the Berlin Schauspielhaus to celebrate the reunion of Germany. The orchestra consisted of musicians from both sides of the former Berlin wall, as well as from the four nations administering the city, and the concert was televised live in more than twenty countries throughout the world. The Ninth Symphony was, of course, on the programme. Before the concert, the conductor, Leonard Bernstein, explained how he had felt authorized 'by the power of the moment' to substitute 'Freiheit' for 'Freude' throughout.

Quinet's description of the Ninth Symphony finale as 'the Marseillaise of humanity' initiated a tradition of French interpretation[51] that continued in 1905 with Georges Pioch's description of the 'Ode to Joy' as 'the Marseillaise of the regenerated and brotherly societies which are to come'.[52] For Quinet and Pioch, the Ninth Symphony was not German; it belonged to the world. In fact during the First World War, in 1915, Camille Mauclair claimed that it belonged to all the world *except* Germany; 'the "Ode to Joy"', he wrote, 'is the unique hymn of the Allies, the credo of all our just hopes, and it would be necessary to forbid criminal Germany ever to play a single bar out of it.'[53] But the peace-makers availed themselves of the Ninth Symphony, too. In 1927, after the foundation of the League of Nations, Édouard Herriot wrote: 'I try to imagine what a celebration it could have been if, after the protocol of Geneva had been signed by all nations, the Ninth Symphony should have sounded among us, as fulfillment and not as mere hope.'[54] It was in France, then, that the foundations were laid for the special role the Ninth Symphony has today as a symbol of Western democracy – a role which Bernstein's performance in Berlin exemplifies almost to the point of banality.

But democracy has no monopoly on the Ninth Symphony. In 1938 a performance under Hermann Abendroth was one of the high points of the Düsseldorf *Reichsmusiktage*, which was intended to become an annual showpiece of Nazi musical culture; in 1942 Furtwängler conducted a performance as part of Hitler's birthday celebrations.[55] The best documented association of the Ninth Symphony with totalitarianism, however, comes from the People's Republic of China. An extended controversy developed out of accusations, made at the time of the Cultural Revolution, that Beethoven's music – and the Ninth Symphony above all – represented capitalist, and therefore reactionary, values. For instance, Ma Ting Heng wrote in 1965 that 'If you listen to more Western bourgeois classical music, it slowly muddles your class viewpoint for understanding problems.' And he cited the finale of the Ninth Symphony as a particular example of this, on the grounds that it holds out the illusion that a progressive and just society can be achieved

95

without class conflict.[56] Against this background, Yan Bao Yu wrote an article in which he attempted to situate both the Ninth Symphony and Schiller's 'An die Freude' in their historical context.[57]

In this article, which dates from 1979, Yan argues that the capitalist ideal of humanism, as embodied in Schiller's poem and Beethoven's music, represented a step forward from the prevailing feudalism of Germany and the Austro-Hungarian empire. Under such circumstances, he says, 'capitalist humanists can be said to be the allies of the proletariat.' And he backs up his case by citing the 'An die Freiheit' story (he knows about this from Grove). He admits that there is doubt as to whether the story is true, but argues that 'in view of Schiller's background and experience, as well as the content of the poem, substituting "Freedom" for "Joy" is basically acceptable and reasonable'. Yan puts forward a similar argument regarding the God of Schiller's text. 'We should not make the mistake of over-simplification', he says, 'and say that all theological thinking in history is reactionary.' Beethoven believed in God, but not in the personalized god of Christianity: he believed in Nature and the principle of moral strength. And whereas Schiller, as he grew older, became caught up in idealist metaphysics, Beethoven remained 'deeply rooted in life and the people on this earth'. This is proved, says Yan, by the simple, joyful nature of the 'Joy' theme – in a word, by its folk-like quality.

In saying this, Yan places himself in a tradition of interpretation that goes back to Wagner, who described the 'Joy' melody as a folksong, and Marx (Adolph, not Karl), who called it a 'simple people's melody'.[58] But there is a more direct influence upon his thinking at this point: Romain Rolland, whose little book *Beethoven* came out in Chinese translation the same year as Yan's article. Rolland's book was originally published in 1903, and it sparked off the extraordinary cult of Beethoven that flourished in France up to the First World War.[59] Rolland presented Beethoven as a beacon of hope in a world that had lost its spiritual values, and the Ninth Symphony is the linchpin of his interpretation. The setting of 'An die Freude', says Rolland, 'was the plan of his whole life'. Rolland quotes from the *Heiligenstadt Testament*, the document in which Beethoven unleashed his despair at the onset of deafness: 'O Providence, grant that but a single day of real happiness may be mine once again. I have been a stranger to the thrill of joy for so long. When, O God, when shall I feel joy once more?. . . Ever again? No, that would be too cruel!'[60] He quotes, too, from the letter to Countess Erdödy in which Beethoven wrote that 'the best of us obtain joy through suffering'.[61] For Rolland, this phrase, 'JOY THROUGH SUFFERING', was 'the motto of his whole heroic soul', and the ultimate message of the Ninth Symphony.

Yan adopts Rolland's idea of the 'An die Freude' setting representing the plan of Beethoven's life; he describes it as the summarizing product of Beethoven's thoughts and experiences. But what is much more important for the Chinese interpretation of the Ninth Symphony is the affinity between Rolland's motto, 'Joy through suffering', and the Marxist slogan, 'Victory through struggle'. If the two are equated, the Ninth Symphony can be fully subsumed within the ideology of Chinese Communism. Yan quotes Rolland's 'Joy through suffering', but stops short of identifying it with 'Victory through struggle'; in arguing the need for a historical understanding of the Ninth Symphony, his intention seems to have been to keep the work at one remove from present-day political interpretations. Other writers, however, explicitly identify the two slogans, and accordingly interpret the Ninth Symphony in directly Marxist terms. Liu Nai Xiong, for instance, writes that 'According to the view of historical materialism, Beethoven in no way intended to advocate reconciliation between the classes through his Ninth Symphony, nor did he intend to contradict the anti-feudalistic spirit of the people. On the contrary, the entire work (including the choral finale) keeps on expressing the spirit of revolutionary struggle.'[62]

Consuming the Ninth

The Japanese reception of the Ninth Symphony (or *Daiku*, as they call it) presents a total contrast to what happened in China. If the Chinese politicized the symphony, the Japanese socialized it. Again Romain Rolland plays an important role in the story; his book was translated into Japanese as early as the 1920s,[63] and prompted an enduring personality cult of the composer. In 1970 the critic Yoshida Hidekazu, who taught at a private university, wrote an article called 'Beethoven Today'. He explained how for the last twenty years he had asked his students to write an essay on music as their final project. Almost all of the students, says Yoshida, chose to write about Beethoven: 'Beethoven has assumed something of the stature of a national hero.' Why is this? Yoshida quotes Rolland's motto, 'Joy through suffering', and adds, 'Students find this philosophy deeply moving.'[64]

But the Ninth Symphony seems to have had a special role in Japan well before the period of which Yoshida speaks. In 1944, it was performed at a concert given in honour of Tokyo University students joining the war: the Ninth Symphony, said one of the organizers, epitomized their desire 'to carry to the battlefield memories of something close to us, something that symbolized our homeland'.[65] And it was even earlier, in 1940, that Joseph

Rosenstock, the chief conductor of the NHK Orchestra, instituted the Japanese custom of performing the Ninth Symphony on 31 December, to mark the end of the year.[66] This custom has nowadays spread to the extent that there are performances of the Ninth Symphony at the year's end, and at other times, all over Japan. Many of these performances are on a massive scale. Choirs of 3,000 or 5,000 are not uncommon; a performance in 1983 had a choir of 7,000. The amateur choirs taking part in these events sometimes train for months.

Events such as these, which spill out of the concert hall into sports halls and stadiums, are primarily social in character. Yano Junichi says that as

the baritone bursts out "Freude!" (joy) and the chorus echoes the word back, listeners in their seats are inwardly singing "Freude!" as well. The conductor, instrumentalists, chorus members, soloists and audience all participate equally in the performance. And therein lies, it seems to me, the secret of the intimacy and harmony between the music of Beethoven and the spiritual life of the Japanese.

It is entirely in the spirit of the Japanese reception of the Ninth Symphony, then, that the finale is available as a karaoke disc;[67] there is even a comic book telling the story of the first performance of the symphony in Japan, at the Bandô prisoner-of-war camp in 1918. We could say that while the Chinese have written about the interpretation of the Ninth Symphony, the Japanese have absorbed it into the fabric of their lives.

For Theodor Adorno, the sociologist and critic who studied composition with Berg and wrote extensively on music, the Ninth Symphony is the prime example of a work destroyed through social usage. Adorno approached music primarily in terms of its relation to society. As he saw it, there was a brief period around the time of the French Revolution when the ideal of freedom was both plausible and realistic, because it seemed possible to reach a mutual accommodation between the interests of the individual and those of society. Beethoven, said Adorno, gave full expression to this ideal in the works of his middle period (to which the first eight symphonies belong); the organic relation of part and whole in Beethoven's music of this period reflects the common interests of individual and society. But the ideal of freedom was betrayed by Napoleon, and terminated by the reimposition of authoritarian rule throughout Europe following the Congress of Vienna. No balance between the interests of the individual and those of society was now possible.

And it is this, says Adorno, that is reflected by the music of Beethoven's third and last period – by its lack of organic unity, its fragmentary quality, its ultimate refusal to make sense. Adorno saw the *Missa solemnis* as the paradigm of such music: by virtue of its hermetic quality and use of archaic devices, he says, it negates 'virtually every characteristic of Beethoven's own earlier style', and so embodies 'the total alienation of Beethoven from his own work'.[68] In this way it resists being subsumed within what Adorno calls 'affirmative culture' – the false culture that proclaims freedom but is in fact an instrument of repression. But the Ninth Symphony is quite different. Adorno's statements about it are contradictory, but the general message is clear: in his urge to communicate with his audience – to smash the communications barrier, as Kerman put it – Beethoven made the work all too intelligible. Whereas the *Missa solemnis* resists interpretation, and so retains its authenticity, the Ninth Symphony has, in effect, been interpreted out of existence. It has been swallowed up by ideology. It has been consumed by social usage.

The force of Adorno's charge cannot be denied:

K.K. Koo III, a young Huppy [Hong Kong upwardly mobile] advertising executive, saw his dream of success one Sunday morning as he waited for a taxi: A white Rolls Royce, chauffeur-driven, with a Chinese man in the back seat soared by. Leaning against the window, the passenger talked intently on a mobile phone. . . . Beethoven's Symphony No. 9 trickled out an open window as a single digit licence number barreled down Tai Hang Road, K.K.'s eyes glaze over as he describes it.[69]

What other work in the repertory could it have been? The work that symbolizes the pursuit of wealth in Hong Kong and communist orthodoxy in the People's Republic, that stands for Western democracy and forms part of Japan's social fabric – how can such a work be said to mean anything at all?

Beyond interpretation?

Political interpretations of music substitute themselves for the original. Implicitly or explicitly, they claim to embody the work *as it is*, leaving no room for doubt or even for personal interpretation. And this is equally true of Wagner's and Schenker's interpretations of the Ninth Symphony. Both Wagner and Schenker lay claim to Beethoven's personal authority, justifying their interpretations by frequent reference to his intentions. In Iser's sense, Wagner and Schenker interpret the Ninth as propaganda no less than do Edgar Quinet or Liu Nai Xiong. But, of course, the very multiplicity of these interpretations undermines their claim to present the work 'as it is'. In reality Beethoven did not write propaganda; Wagner, Schenker, Quinet, and Liu have all inserted their interpretations into the gaps in his music, so consummating, so to speak, Beethoven's symbols. This corresponds to Iser's second model of musical meaning. But from the perspective of Adorno's critique, the difference between Iser's first and second models does not count for that much. By substituting itself for the original, a dominant interpretation can turn the work into propaganda. And that is what Adorno says has happened to the Ninth Symphony.

But at this point I would like to put forward the third model of musical meaning to which I referred in chapter 5. *Parsifal* is a prime example of this. It is obvious that *Parsifal* is about compassion: the relationship between the first and last acts is precisely that Parsifal lacks this quality in the first act but has acquired it in the last. To this extent, it is a human drama, a drama about personal development. But there are elements in *Parsifal* that are entirely incompatible with this, such as the prophecy from the vault of the cathedral and the spear that hovers in mid air. These are clearly symbols of some kind of transcendent force that intrudes upon the human drama. Like Christianity, *Parsifal* asserts that only man can help himself, and that only God can help man; and yet the two assertions are at loggerheads with each other. The result is that *Parsifal* cannot be embraced within any single interpretation. Every interpretation of it is contradicted by the work itself.

I want to suggest that this is the appropriate model for the Ninth Symphony. I want to suggest that the work is profoundly ambivalent, and that its ambivalence is focused round its relationship to Beethoven's earlier music. Many commentators have remarked on the strongly retrospective quality of the Ninth Symphony. It represents a return to the heroic ideals that were adumbrated in the 'Leopold' Cantata of 1790 (where Beethoven first set the words 'Stürzet nieder, Millionen') and subsequently developed in the 'Eroica' Symphony and other works of his middle period. The finale harks back to the *Choral Fantasy* of 1808, in terms of both general conception and structural features; Beethoven repeatedly referred to the similarities between the two works in letters to publishers.[1] And both the Ninth Symphony and the *Choral Fantasy* are reminiscent of the French Revolutionary music of the 1790s, when massed choirs and orchestras took part in outdoor ceremonies.

Above all, the very idea of setting 'An die Freude' – an idea which never seems to have been far from Beethoven's mind – represents some kind of reversion to the libertarian thinking of the 1780s, when Schiller wrote his poem. In a speech written around the same time, Schiller described universal love as 'the bond that unites all men' and spoke of an eternal law that 'establishes a correlation between individual happiness and the perfection of society'.[2] These words closely anticipate Adorno's characterization of the brief period when it was possible to believe in freedom. And 'An die Freude' was one of the foremost symbols of this period. As Bernt von Heiseler says,

> from the first moment of its existence, this whole age, with its enthusiasm and belief in man, recognized its own reflection in it, an age on the eve of the Great Revolution, which wanted to change everything and create a paradise on earth. Transcripts were circulated even before the poem was printed. . . . It was sung wherever young people came together.[3]

But, as Adorno said, the ideals for which it stood were comprehensively betrayed by Napoleon and the Congress of Vienna. Schiller himself obtained a patent of nobility in 1802, and in the following year published a revised version of 'An die Freude' in which some of the more overtly political lines were toned down:[4] for instance, the seventh line, 'Beggars shall be the brothers of princes', became 'All men shall be brothers'. The poet Bernt von Kleist made what von Heiseler calls a 'terrible retraction' of 'An die Freude', writing an ode in the same metre and verse form, which depicts

> the misery and scorn which the foreigners have inflicted upon his nation, and in place of the praise of joy 'which all beings drink' there now stands hatred expressed in the wild exaggeration of ghastly images. It is frightening to compare the two odes in detail

and to see how, in passage after passage, the later poet answers the earlier in a gloomy litany.[5]

And it is in the same sense that we are to understand the retraction of the Ninth Symphony in Thomas Mann's *Doctor Faustus*. Adrian Leverkühn, the composer and protagonist of the novel, is speaking:

'I find', he said, 'that it is not to be.'

'What Adrian, is not to be?'

'The good and noble,' he answered me; 'what we call the human, although it is good, and noble. What human beings have fought for and stormed citadels, what the ecstatics exultantly announced – that is not to be. It will be taken back. I will take it back.'

'I don't quite understand, dear man. What will you take back?'

'The Ninth Symphony,' he replied. And then no more came, though I waited for it.[6]

Thomas Mann consulted frequently with Adorno while writing *Doctor Faustus*, and it is generally assumed that many of the views expressed in the novel are to be ascribed to Adorno.[7] Certainly Leverkühn, like Adorno, seems to see the Ninth Symphony as the great symbol of affirmative culture. That is how most people see it. Basil Deane, for instance, calls the symphony a 'reaffirmation of the youthful idealism which remained unshaken by thirty disillusioning years'.[8] But can Beethoven really have been so unthinking, so *dumb*, as to remain unaffected by the history of his own time, holding true to the beliefs of the 1780s in the Vienna of the 1820s, with its censorship, secret police, and network of informers? Deane's interpretation reduces the Ninth Symphony to woolly optimism or Hollywood-style escapism. Solomon insists that such interpretations are necessary; 'if we lose our awareness of the transcendent realms of play, beauty, and brotherhood which are portrayed in the great affirmative works of our culture,' he says, 'if we lose the dream of the Ninth Symphony, there remains no counterpoise against the engulfing terrors of civilization, nothing to set against Auschwitz and Vietnam as a paradigm of humanity's potentialities.'[9] But in referring to the Ninth Symphony as a 'dream', Solomon comes dangerously close to saying that we need something to believe in, even if we don't believe in it.

Beethoven's contemporaries often commented on the way in which he juxtaposed incongruous elements and moods in his music. In 1811, following a performance of the first two symphonies, Giuseppe Cambini wrote that

The composer Beethoven, often bizarre and baroque, sometimes sparkles with extraordinary beauties. Now he takes the majestic flight of the eagle; then he creeps along grotesque paths. After penetrating the soul with a sweet melancholy he soon tears it by a mass of barbaric chords. He seems to harbour doves and crocodiles at the same time.[10]

And Rey Longyear associates these incongruities with the plays of Ludwig Tieck, which (as Longyear puts it) juxtapose 'the ultraserious with the ironic or even with slapstick comedy, the poetic with the prosaic, and commonplace reality with flights of imagination'.[11] Tieck writes what, following Treitler, we could call drama interpreted by itself: actors planted in the audience interrupt the action, the producer and prompter appear on stage, and at the end of one of his plays the playwright 'is driven from the stage by a barrage of paper wads and spoiled fruit'. And the purpose of all this? To represent the author's detachment from his work, says Longyear, and to destroy illusion.

The juxtaposition of the ultraserious and slapstick: I can think of no better description of bar 331 of the Ninth Symphony finale, the beginning of the 'Turkish' music, where the majestic tones of 'And the seraph stands with God' are punctuated by the 'absurd grunts' (some people have called them farts[12]) of the bassoons and bass drum. At this point Beethoven's music deconstructs Schiller's text. Or maybe Schiller's text deconstructs itself; the juxtaposition of the worm and the seraph is in itself incongruous enough. Either way, the affirmative message is, if not denied, then undermined; to borrow Longyear's formulation, Beethoven detaches himself from it, suggests that it may be illusory. And the same applies to other moments of incongruity in the finale. One is bars 843–50, which link the sublimely elaborate cadenza of bars 832–42 to the final *Prestissimo*. To Beethoven, the link passage can't have sounded like Offenbach's *Orpheus in the Underworld*; but it must have sounded like Rossini, the composer whose music had swept Vienna in 1822–3, and whom Schindler blamed for the final decline of serious music. Another moment of incongruity, perhaps, is the double fugue that begins at bar 655, superimposing a variant of the 'Joy' theme upon the 'Seid umschlungen' theme. This can be seen as the climactic synthesis of two of the most disparate elements of the finale. But it can also be seen as a purposely exaggerated display of technical virtuosity that intrudes upon the message of both text and music.

Perhaps the most explicit technique of Beethoven's irony is anachronism. The extended sections in a kind of synthetic plainsong – Cooper's 'Gregorian fossils' – might possibly be regarded as unequivocal statements of simple, unquestioning faith; faith was already associated with the antique in Beethoven's day. But the repeated turning of the music towards the end to an anachronistic Mozartean style cannot be explained this way. As the choir sing 'All men shall be brothers', in bar 810, they slip out of Beethoven's style and into that of the 1780s; as the verbal expression reaches maximum intensity, the music goes into quotation marks. Nothing could more clearly express Beethoven's detachment from his own message; nothing could more clearly indicate the retrospective, and therefore ultimately futile, nature of the Enlightenment ideals that Schiller's words proclaim.

Less explicit, but more unnerving, is the music to which Beethoven sets the passages from Schiller's text that affirm the Creator's presence: 'Brothers! above the canopy of the stars There must dwell a loving Father! . . . Beyond the stars he must dwell' (bars 619–26, 650–54). Everyone finds these passages affecting, especially the second. Grove says it is 'full of mystery and devotion', while Hopkins describes it as 'a moment of extraordinary magic'. For Cooper it is like being 'poised at an infinite space above the earth, bathed in starlight and on the brink of some great revelation'. Tovey calls it 'the central thought of the Ninth Symphony', Treitler calls it 'the dénouement of the whole symphony'.[13] And it seems likely Beethoven thought of it in much the same way, given the famous words that he jotted down in a conversation book of 1820: 'The moral law within us and the starry sky above us – Kant!!!'[14]

The meaning of Schiller's text is plain; but what is the meaning of the music to which Beethoven set it? Solomon hears bars 619–26 as

a heart-rending question mark. . . . The chorus's measured rhythmic unison disintegrates on the word 'muss' [must], which is sounded successively by the basses, the tenors and altos, and finally by the sopranos, as though by repeated emphasis to query what they dare not acknowledge in reality, that the multitudes have been embracing before an absent deity, *Deus absconditus*.[15]

Maybe it takes a twentieth-century listener to hear the music this way; inevitably, Solomon is reading his own concerns and values into Beethoven's music. But his final words seem the more telling as applied to bars 650–54, for here the music is the very embodiment of cosmic emptiness.

Beethoven's last symphony proclaims the ideals of universal brotherhood and joy; that is unmistakable. But at the same time, and just as unmistakably, it casts doubt upon them. It sends out incompatible messages. And that is why, like *Parsifal*, the Ninth Symphony has the capacity to resist being wholly assimilated within any single, definitive interpretation; however it is interpreted, there is always a remainder that lies beyond interpretation. But this resistance can only be effective if we remain conscious of the incongruities, the incoherence, the negative qualities of the music. Grove heard these things, but their message was incompatible with his Victorian values and so he discounted them:

If in the *Finale* a restless, boisterous spirit occasionally manifests itself, not in keeping with the English feeling of the solemnity, even the sanctity, of the subject, this is only a reflection, and by no means an exaggerated reflection, of the bad taste which is manifested in parts of the lines adopted from Schiller's Ode, and which Beethoven, no doubt, thought it was his duty to carry out in the music.[16]

For listeners today, the danger is of simply not hearing such things. This is partly the result of today's 'brilliant, glossy, "official" performances', as Adorno called them, that 'smooth over any discontinuities which might jolt the listener'.[17] But the basic problem is perhaps that we have heard the Ninth Symphony too often. 'The more time we spend in the presence of [Beethoven's] music,' observes Steinberg, 'the harder it is truly to hear it.'[18]

And that is why hearing it is not enough. As Treitler says, 'The critical task is to interpret the text again (and again and again)'.[19] This task is critical not just in the sense that critics do it, but that it is the only way to prevent the Ninth Symphony from being consumed by ideology. If we are to be successful in this, however, we will have to keep before us (as Wagner did not) the image of a Beethoven who was both earnest and ironical.

APPENDIX 1

Schiller's 'An die Freude' and the Ninth Symphony

Beethoven seems to have had the setting of Friedrich Schiller's 'An die Freude' in mind throughout most of his life. Thayer quotes a letter written by Bartolomäus Fischenich in 1793 in which he mentions Beethoven's intention of setting 'An die Freude' (*Thayer's Life*, pp. 120–21), and there is some evidence that Beethoven actually did make a setting of it around 1798, though if so it has been lost; other notes relating to the text date from 1811–12 (Brandenburg, 'Die Skizzen', pp. 89–90).

Schiller originally wrote 'An die Freude' in 1785. But in 1803 he published a revised version in which some of the more explicitly political passages of the earlier version were toned down. Beethoven drew on the 1803 version for his Ninth Symphony, setting the first three verses and the first, third, and fourth choruses. He omitted those sections of the poem that turn it into an 'elevated drinking song', as Solomon puts it (*Beethoven*, p. 434). And he reorders the choruses in such a way that the initial picture of universal rejoicing (verses 1–3) is followed by the image of the hero speeding through the heavens (chorus 4); only after that does Beethoven introduce the choruses that depict the Creator beyond the stars (choruses 1, 3). In this way he creates a continuous line of development from the terrestrial to the divine.

Choruses 1 and 3 represent the spiritual kernel of Beethoven's setting, and after they first appear (bar 595) he uses only them and the first verse, sometimes in alternation, and at one point simultaneously (in the double fugue, bar 655). From this point on the setting becomes increasingly fragmented and impressionistic, with individual lines or even words ('Freude!') being picked out and absorbed within the musical texture. This upset a number of contemporary critics; a review of the 1826 Leipzig performance, for instance, complained that 'isolated strophes follow one another in an entirely changed order, like fragments that the composer by chance found in his memory' (Levy, 'Early performances', p. 361).

At the first English performance, in 1825, the text was sung in Italian; the reasons for this are not clear (Levy, p. 160). A number of English translations were used thereafter, many of which seem to have located the work in the English oratorio tradition; critics refer to such numbers as 'Welcome ye', 'Awake the tuneful measure', and 'Glory be thine eternal nature'. By the end of the century, Natalia MacFarren's two translations had supplanted the others. The earlier one is printed in Grove's book; Tovey gives the later one, which is still to be found in miniature scores of the symphony. Ruth Solie has analyzed the way in which the earlier version bowdlerizes Schiller's text by de-emphasizing pagan elements in favour of orthodox Christianity. A representative example is the third chorus, where Schiller's interrogatives are replaced by what Solie calls 'hortatory statements direct from the pulpit' ('Beethoven as secular humanist', p. 35):

> Oh ye millions, kneel before Him,
> Tremble, earth, before thy Lord.
> Mercy holds his flashing sword,
> As our father we implore Him!

The second line has an authoritarian tone which is not present in Schiller's text, while the third and fourth lines bear no relation to the original; MacFarren introduces the Christian concept of 'Mercy' in place of Schiller's cosmic imagery, and eliminates the profession of belief (or hope?) in the last line. The later version is closer to the original text:

> Oh ye millions kneel before Him,
> World, dost feel thy Maker near?
> Seek Him o'er yon starry sphere,
> O'er the stars enthron'd, adore Him!

But the hortatory tone of the last line remains; and as Tovey points out, the whole stanza still 'reverses Schiller's and Beethoven's conception, the point of which is *not* to fall prostrate, but to rise from prostration and look upwards to the Father above the starry vault' ('Ninth Symphony', p. 124). The general trend of both MacFarren translations, then, is to substitute an institutionalized Christianity for the humanistic freedom expressed by the original text.

The following includes only those sections of Schiller's text that Beethoven set. The numbering of the verses and choruses, however, refers to the full text.

Verse 1
Freude, schöner Götterfunken, Tochter aus Elysium,
Wir betreten feuertrunken, Himmlische, dein Heiligtum.
Deine Zauber binden wieder, Was die Mode streng geteilt;
Alle Menschen werden Brüder, Wo dein sanfter Flügel weilt.

Verse 2
Wem der grosse Wurf gelungen, Eines Freundes Freund zu sein,
Wer ein holdes Weib errungen, Mische seinen Jubel ein!
Ja – wer auch nur eine Seele Sein nennt auf dem Erdenrund!
Und wer's nie gekonnt, der stehle Weinend sich aus diesem Bund.

Verse 3
Freude trinken alle Wesen An den Brüsten der Natur;
Alle Guten, alle Bösen Folgen ihrer Rosenspur.
Küsse gab sie uns und Reben, Einen Freund, geprüft im Tod;
Wollust ward dem Wurm gegeben, Und der Cherub steht vor Gott.

Chorus 4
Froh, wie seine Sonnen fliegen Durch des Himmels prächt'gen Plan,
Laufet, Brüder, eure Bahn, Freudig wie ein Held zum Siegen.

Chorus 1
Seid umschlungen, Millionen! Diesen Kuss der ganzen Welt!
Brüder – überm Sternenzelt Muss ein lieber Vater wohnen.

Chorus 3
Ihr stürzt nieder, Millionen? Ahnest du den Schöpfer, Welt?
Such ihn überm Sternenzelt! Über Sternen muss er wohnen.

Joy, beautiful spark of the gods, daughter of Elysium,
Intoxicated with your fire, heavenly one, we enter your shrine.
Your magic power reunites what strict custom has divided;
All men become brothers where your gentle wing rests.

Whoever has the great good fortune to enjoy mutual friendship,
Whoever has taken a loving wife, let him join us in celebration!
Yes! Even he who has nothing to call his own but his soul!
But he who cannot rejoice, let him steal weeping away.

All creatures partake of joy at Nature's breast;
Nature nourishes all that is good or evil,
Dispensing kisses and wine to us, a friend tested in death.
The worm is in ecstasy, and the cherub stands before God.

Brothers, go on your way as glad as the stars as they hurtle
Through the heavens, as joyful as a hero on his way to triumph.

Be embraced, you millions! Here's a kiss for all the world!
Brothers! above the canopy of the stars there must dwell a loving Father!

Do you fall to your knees, you millions? World, do you sense your Maker?
Seek him beyond the stars! Beyond the stars he must dwell!

The text of the Ninth Symphony

by JONATHAN DEL MAR *(Editor, Hanover Band Urtext Edition, 1988)*

The sources

There is, at the time of writing, no authoritative published score of the Ninth Symphony. All editions in common use contain inaccuracies and even bowdlerized versions of what Beethoven wrote, an unfortunate situation compounded by the complexity of the sources for the work. These sources are as follows:

A Autograph score, housed in the Staatsbibliothek zu Berlin, with the exception of the following sections (all, except IV 650–54, composed later):
  in the Beethovenhaus, Bonn: II 926–54
  in the Bibliothèque Nationale, Paris: IV 343–75
  lost: IV 650–54, 814–21
A facsimile of the Autograph was published by Kistner & Siegel in 1924, and reprinted by Edition Peters in 1975.

AP Autograph parts:
  in the Beethovenhaus, Bonn: trombones (just the parts lacking in A, i.e. 1st and 2nd
    for II, and all three for IV 655–940)
  in the Staatsbibliothek zu Berlin: contrabassoon.

PX Nine manuscript string parts (three each of Vl 1, Vl 2, VcB) from the original material used at the first performance; housed in the library of the Gesellschaft der Musikfreunde, Vienna. All have a few corrections in Beethoven's hand.

B Copyist's score, with Beethoven's corrections, the property of the Royal Philharmonic Society, but on loan to the British Library, London. This score was used at the performance on 21 March 1825.

C Copyist's score used as engraver's copy (Stichvorlage) for E, P, V (see below), in the archive of B. Schotts Söhne, Mainz. C is in fact two sources in one. In its original form it was written by two copyists and was taken directly from A, probably in March 1824. Into this score Beethoven entered a vast amount of revision and correction, prior to the copying from it of PX and then B. After this it was in quite a mess, and Beethoven had the worst pages recopied by four other copyists. These replacement pages (C') have hardly any corrections by Beethoven, and contain new mistakes of their own.

X Pages originally belonging to C which were superseded by C'. These comprise:

Twelve separate sheets in the Staatsbibliothek zu Berlin, containing I 268–77, 413–20; II 491–530; IV 1–8, 233–40, 376–416, 427–36. These are of great interest, as they are seething with corrections by Beethoven and authenticate a large number of differences between A and C', particularly the end of the Trio. These pages were recopied for C' by Ferdinand Wolanek.

One sheet containing IV 417–26 and bound in with A, as folio 121. Beethoven revised these bars to such an extent that he deleted them entirely in A, inserting this sheet instead. The corresponding page in C' was recopied by Wolanek, but at an earlier date than the twelve sheets mentioned above.

Pages still present in the Mainz score, but over which C' has been stuck so that X is usually only partially legible. These comprise I 333–7; II 78–83, 297–302; IV 813/22–5. Sometimes the new page contains one more bar than the old one did, so that the final bar of X is deleted on the next page of C; an example is I 338.

Places where a small patch (sometimes as little as one bar in one instrument) has been struck over X. In such cases X is usually irretrievable.

There are also several whole pages of X that have been lost. These are I 147–54; III 1–9; IV 150–59, 331–42, 487–96, 604–729.

All this means that, as a general rule, anything now in the Mainz score in the hand of any but the original two copyists – i.e. all of C – stems not from A, but from X. The exceptions are the three sections composed later (see A above); in each case C' stems directly from A.

CP Manuscript parts in the archive of B. Schotts Söhne, Mainz:

Three trombone parts, copied from AP, each with a few corrections in Beethoven's hand.

Four chorus parts, copied from C, with no autograph corrections.

Four solo voice parts, with no autograph corrections.

All these parts once formed part of PX, being used at the first performance and later being removed from the set to serve as Stichvorlage parts.

D Copyist's score, in two volumes, in the Stadtarchiv, Aachen.

I–III, with Beethoven's corrections. This volume was sent by Beethoven to Aachen around 12 March 1825; it was used at the performance in the Niederrheinisches Musikfest on 23 May, with Ferdinand Ries conducting.

IV, copied by the Aachen trumpeter Uhlig from DP (see below), with no autograph corrections.

DC Copyist's vocal score, with Beethoven's corrections, in the Stadtarchiv, Aachen. Beethoven sent this score to Aachen on or before 9 April 1825.

DP Manuscript set of parts, used at the 1825 Aachen performance; now lost.

Ex. 19 Relationships between the sources

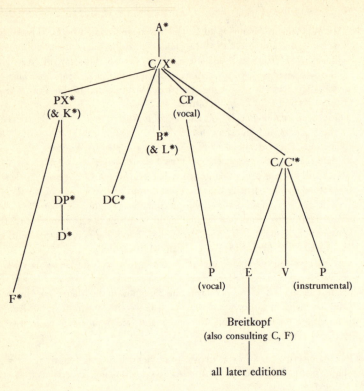

F   Copyist's score, with Beethoven's corrections, in the Staatsbibliothek zu Berlin. This presentation copy, with an autograph dedication to King Friedrich Wilhelm III, was delivered to the King at the end of September 1826.

J   One autograph sheet in the Staatsbibliothek zu Berlin. This originally contained only the four autograph bars I 255–8 missing in A, but was later used by Beethoven as a scribbling pad. It includes some interesting memoranda concerning both the Ninth Symphony and the Missa Solemnis.

K   Correction list in Beethoven's hand, with a few annotations by Wolanek, auctioned at Sotheby's for £85,000 on 6 May 1988 and now in private ownership. Most of the mistakes being corrected were probably copyist's errors in PX.

L   An almost exact copy of K, dated 20 January 1825 and now in the Beethovenhaus, Bonn; largely in Wolanek's hand. This list was prepared for the purpose of ensuring the accuracy of B, and was sent to London on 27 January 1825.

E First edition of full score, published by Schott in August 1826. The proofs were not checked by Beethoven.

V First edition of vocal score, also published by Schott in August 1826.

P First edition of vocal and instrumental parts, published by Schott simultaneously with E and V.

Ex. 19 shows the relationships between the different sources; the vertical axis shows the relative chronology of sources, while sources containing autograph corrections are marked with an asterisk.

The relative importance of the sources

A and C are the most important sources. There are certain respects in which C is the more important, because of the vast number of autograph corrections and revisions in it. Furthermore, C is the only copy taken directly from A, and this means that differences between later sources and A can be resolved according to whether or not they originate from Beethoven's corrections in C. When they do not, they are just as likely to be copyist's errors, and no other source gives us any information in this respect.

Like any copyist's score, however, C contains slips. Thus A has to be taken as the primary source throughout, though in many instances not the final one. The central issue in preparing an authoritative edition of the Ninth Symphony is when to follow A and when to follow C. The differences between A and C can be divided into seven categories, in order of increasing complexity:

Places where A gives an earlier version, revised by Beethoven in C. Here there is no problem.

Specific corrections in K. Again, no problem.

Places where Beethoven's revisions are in X. Where we have X (particularly those pages in the Staatsbibliothek zu Berlin) this is no problem, but sometimes X is hidden beneath C' and cannot be made out. Sometimes whole pages of X are lost, so that we have to make our own judgement, generally on musical grounds, as to whether the reading in C' is likely to have emanated from Beethoven.

Copyist's errors in C. These were quite unusually profuse and multifarious, partly because of the difficulty of reading A, and partly because of the shortcomings of the copyists. Though Beethoven was meticulous in his correction of C, some errors inevitably remained. The simplest to recognize are those where A is ambiguous or hard to decipher, owing to combinations of 8va signs or other forms of shorthand, and notes or dynamics impossibly squeezed in.

Places in A where the text found in C is deleted in favour of a new version. These deletions clearly postdate the copying of C, and some even postdate the first stage of Beethoven's corrections to C; so that we are probably dealing here with revisions that came into Beethoven's mind while C was being used for the copying of either PX or B.

A very few places where the copyist seems originally to have been in doubt, then entered a text different from that in A. These apparently conscious decisions, made independently of A, must derive either from another, lost correction list (which is unlikely, given the existence of both K and L) or from conversations with Beethoven. Records of such conversations in March and April 1824 do exist, but are extremely sparse, and include nothing of immediate textual importance. However there is reason to believe that Schindler destroyed a number of the conversation books after Beethoven's death, and these may have contained such conversations with copyists. Apart from illegible passages, there are a few places in A where the scoring is not quite complete, and the conversations that do survive indicate that copyists were reluctant to fill in or guess at notes that Beethoven did not write.

The most problematic of all are those few instances where the copyists quite simply wrote something different from a palpably clear text in A. They were working under pressure, and now and then simply read the wrong bar or stave, or missed something out. At the same time, instructions from the composer cannot always be ruled out, in most of these cases it is necessary to combine circumstantial evidence with musical judgement in order to decide which text to follow.

All other sources derive directly or indirectly from C, X, or C', and are consequently of subsidiary importance except where they show a correction in Beethoven's hand. There are just two exceptions to this:

Where X is lost, B (and PX, where that survives) is of special significance in deducing what X's text was.

Since most of PX is lost, it is just possible that those readings unique to sources deriving from PX (i.e. D and F) could have emanated from corrections by Beethoven in the lost parts.

Sources of error in E and subsequent editions

Breitkopf und Härtel published a full score of the Ninth Symphony in 1864, as part of the Gesamtausgabe. This was the first serious attempt to undertake a critical edition of the work. But it had flaws. It was based on E; many of the ambiguities and inconsistencies in E were eliminated, but the only other sources consulted were C and F. A, in particular, was ignored. Since the current Peters, Eulenburg, and Philharmonia editions are all based on the 1864 Breitkopf edition, most of the notorious errors to be found in them actually go back to E. Stage by stage, the chief sources of error in this process of transmission were as follows:

The transition from A to C (or X). Over a hundred errors by the copyist slipped through, almost all of which have remained undetected ever since. The most significant departure of the new Hanover Band Urtext edition from all previous ones is that it takes account of the autograph for the first time since C. Until now scholars have assumed that, because Beethoven revised the work in so many respects, the only valid sources for an authoritative edition are the copyists' scores.

But there are many instances where only A has the correct text, and a simple copying error has been transferred from one source or edition to another. For example, at II 352, the timpani part (which should be the same as in bar 111) is hurriedly written in A, so that its last two notes look like rests – for which they have been mistaken ever since.

The recopying of certain pages of C. Beethoven only checked this recopying very cursorily, and many errors remained, most of which were perpetuated in E. At the end of the Trio, for example, Beethoven had added ties between the violins' minims within each bar from 503 to 506 and 515 to 522; but this revision, which Beethoven made in X, was so carelessly reproduced by Wolanek that the Breitkopf editors resorted to an entirely different solution based on a version long since discarded by Beethoven. And that is what is played today.

The transition from C (or C') to E. Beethoven did not supervise this, and literally hundreds of errors were made, though many were later corrected by Breitkopf. Important examples that slipped through the net include the following:

Beethoven frequently writes *piu piano......*, clearly signifying a diminuendo. The continuation marks are all left out in E, so that in places like III 23 we hear an entirely spurious sequence of stepwise dynamics. The same is true at I 492 and III 41, and similarly with the *piu forte.....* at I 527.

III 53, Vl 1, first note: this salient melodic note is D in all authentic sources, misprinted as C in E, and thence in all modern editions and performances.

In the first edition parts the contrabassoon part was rewritten to suit most instruments of the day, which lacked the bottom B♭. Beethoven frequently used this striking note, which was not impossible in his day and is standard practice now. Beethoven's original contrabassoon part is much more colourful and eventful than that normally heard.

The transition from E to the 1864 Breitkopf edition. Very few major errors were made, though many details were overlooked which can now be restored. A paramount error, however, occurred in the flute and oboe at I 81, where the B♭ found in Breitkopf and all modern editions is wrong. All sources read D, a third higher; Beethoven wrote this note in *both* instruments in A, so it can hardly be a mistake (despite the difference in the recapitulation).

Some controversies

We can now look at, and sometimes resolve, a few of the many textual controversies that have raged ever since the Ninth Symphony was published.

I 111, 378 The last two cello notes have often excited curiosity. All sources agree that they are both Bs in 111, but D E♭ in 378. In each case, repetition of the previous bar would have caused consecutive seconds with the melody; Beethoven chose to solve the problem in two different ways.

I 217 Berlioz and Moscheles were both upset by the clash on the first beat between the G and E♭ in the oboes and the A♭ and F in the strings; Moscheles altered the oboe parts, and certain modern editions bowdlerize the text at this point (including the Eulenburg miniature score edited by Max Unger). However the clash is confirmed in all sources.

II 412   The only authentic figure for this ill fated metronome mark is minim = 116, as written down by Beethoven's nephew Karl during his session with Beethoven on 27 September 1826, and copied directly by him, twice, into F. The reading semibreve = 116 is first found in the 1864 Breitkopf edition, and derived from late 1827 printings of E in which the tail of the minim at the top of the page had been worn away (though the one below the staves remained intact). But musical sense suggests that minim = 116 cannot be correct either, because of the *stringendo* to the Presto. It is possible that the correct marking is minim = 160, and that the confusion resulted from the similarity between 'sixteen' and 'sixty' (equally similar in German). Equally, it may be that Karl failed to catch the figure of the Trio, and gestured to Ludwig who did not realize what Karl was asking and repeated the figure for the Scherzo instead. If that is what happened, what Karl wrote down is simply wrong, and the true metronome mark of the Trio is irretrievably lost.

IV 115   One of the outstanding controversies of the symphony. There is no doubt that Beethoven intended the second bassoon to play from the fourth beat, though it was an afterthought; the only mystery is how he forgot to make the correction in C. In A there is a later pencil correction '2do Fag col B'; B has 'Fag. 2do sempre coi Bassi' and 'Fag.2/c.B' in the margin, both in Beethoven's hand; both D and F have the entire double bass part written out in a separate stave for the second bassoon. Moreover, in F Beethoven corrected a missing tie in just this part. Only in C is there no sign of the emendation, which is why it was omitted in E, the 1864 Breitkopf edition, and all other editions. The omission is particularly surprising because Beethoven wrote 'Contrafag. tacet' in this very bar of C; one would have thought that, had he wanted the second bassoon here, he would have noticed its absence. However, the very fact of his writing 'Contrafag. tacet' shows that he assumed the presence of the second bassoon, since the last instruction for the contrabassoon was 'col 2.Fag'; if the second bassoon were not meant to be playing here, there would have been no need for the new contrabassoon marking.

IV 221   The baritone's first note is F, but it should be sung as G in the usual tradition of vocal appoggiaturas. In A, the G is deleted in favour of F; but this was surely a notational revision, not a musical one. Interestingly enough, the G (slurred to F) is found in B where, on the stave below the original, the whole phrase is written out with English translation. This could have been added some years later, since the first London performance was sung in Italian; all the same, it helps confirm that the note actually sung in performances at the time was G, matching bar 16. But the most persuasive evidence is found in the sketches, where bars 80–90 appear as a vocal solo, with the first note of bar 84 being accordingly written as F♯ (*Thayer's Life*, p. 894).

IV 758   Another clash, this time between the C♮ in the woodwind and the C♯ in the altos and violas; it has been 'corrected' by such interpreters as Moscheles (who altered the C♯ to C♮) and Schenker (who altered the C♮ to C♯). As in the case of I 217, all sources agree, and all editions preserve the authentic text except Unger's Eulenburg miniature score.

IV 823 Wagner and Grove were both passionate advocates of the reading *frech* (cheeky, impudent) which C', E, and V have in place of *streng* (stern, strict). But as Otto Baensch demonstrated, the source of this reading was an error by the copyist of C'; in the Gothic script prevalent at the time, *frech* looks remarkably like *streng*. Proof of the authenticity of *streng* is found in DC, where this very word came under Beethoven's scrutiny. He altered it from *streng–* to *stre–ng*.

Notes

Preface

1 Claude-Achille Debussy, *M. Croche the Dilettant Hater* (London, 1927), p. 29.
2 F. J. Crowest, *Beethoven* (London, 1899), p. 199.
3 Robert Schumann, *On Music and Musicians*, ed. Konrad Wolf, trans. Paul Rosenfeld (New York, 1969), p. 98.
4 Ibid., pp. 100–101.
5 Quoted in David Levy, 'Early performances of Beethoven's Ninth Symphony: a documentary study of five cities' (Ph.D. diss., Eastman School of Music, Rochester, 1979), p. 391. Except when otherwise cited, extracts from nineteenth century press reports in this book are taken from this source. Levy quotes the original texts in full and provides bibliographic information. The translations given here are based on Levy's.
6 See *The Beethoven Newsletter*, 4/3 (Spring 1989), p. 23.

1 Sketches and myths

1 For details see Sieghard Brandenburg, 'Die Skizzen zur neunten Symphonie', in Harry Goldschmidt (ed.), *Zur Beethoven 2: Aufsätze und Dokumente* (Berlin, 1984), pp. 88–129. The transcription in Ex. 2 is taken from pp. 95–6. Square brackets indicate editorial additions in this and other sketch transcriptions.
2 Gustav Nottebohm, 'Skizzen zur neunten Symphonie', in *Zweite Beethoveniana: nachgelassene Aufsätze* (Leipzig, 1887), pp. 157–92. The transcriptions from Boldrini are from p. 158 (last two examples) to p. 162.
3 Ex. 4 is taken from Brandenburg, 'Die Skizzen', p. 97. Brandenburg argues that this sheet may originally have been part of Autograph 11/1, which Beethoven used from late 1816 to late 1817 or early 1818 (p. 99).
4 Mendelssohn 2, p. 94, transcribed in Brandenburg, 'Die Skizzen', p. 102. Brandenburg believes that this leaf is from Vienna A44, indicating a date of summer 1818.
5 For details of the commission, see Pamela Willetts, *Beethoven and England: an Account of Sources in the British Museum* (London, 1970), pp. 44ff.
6 Bar 29 of the Engelmann version also relates back to the penultimate bar of the Mainz version (Ex. 4), which has the same G–F–E figure in diminution.
7 The fullest account of the first movement sketches is Jenny Kallick, 'A study of the advanced sketches and full score autograph for the first movement of Beethoven's Ninth Symphony, Opus 125' (Ph.D. diss., Yale University, 1987).

8 George Grove, *Beethoven and his Nine Symphonies* (London, 1896), p. 326.
9 Transcription from Brandenburg, 'Die Skizzen', p. 96. The evidence for the date is that there are sketches for 'Das Schweigen' on p. 55 of Scheide.
10 Published in the Supplement to the *Beethoven Gesamtausgabe*, vol. 6, p. 147.
11 Nicholas Marston, 'Beethoven's "anti-organicism"? The origins of the slow movement of the Ninth Symphony', in *Studies in the History of Music 3: The Compositional Process* (New York, forthcoming).
12 Ex. 9 is taken from Marston; the original is in the Beethovenhaus, Bonn (BSk 20, fol. 1ʳ). Barry Cooper uses this material in his speculative reconstruction of a 'Tenth Symphony'. Its resemblance to the slow movement of the 'Pathétique' Sonata hardly needs pointing out.
13 The transcription is again taken from Marston. Landsberg 8 is the most important sketchbook for the later part of the composition of the Ninth Symphony.
14 Ex. 11 is taken from Landsberg 8/2, p. 77 (transcribed in Nottebohm, 'Skizzen', p. 177).
15 BSk 8/56 in the Beethovenhaus, Bonn; see Brandenburg, 'Die Skizzen', p. 103.
16 Elliot Forbes (ed.), *Thayer's Life of Beethoven* (Princeton, 1967), p. 888. The actual authorship of some of the material in *Thayer's Life* is hard to determine, but in what follows I shall refer to it as being all by Thayer.
17 Brandenburg's reading ('Die Skizzen', p. 109) of the passage Nottebohm marked with dots is 'as in the A♭ sonata' (i.e. Op. 110).
18 Quoted in Anton Schindler, *Beethoven as I Knew Him* (New York, 1972), p. 269.
19 See Maynard Solomon, 'Beethoven's creative process: a two-part invention', in *Beethoven Essays* (Cambridge, 1988). This paragraph is based on p. 136.
20 The reading 'trombones' is Robert Winter's; see his 'The sketches for the "Ode to Joy"', in Robert Winter and Bruce Carr (eds.), *Beethoven, Performers, and Critics* (Detroit, 1980), p. 180.
21 See the discussion in Brandenburg, 'Die Skizzen', p. 109.
22 Nottebohm, 'Skizzen', p. 180; Winter ('The sketches', p. 197) putatively reads 'also' (*auch*) after 'however'. The sources of Nottebohm's four transcriptions are, respectively, Landsberg 8/2, p. 37; Aut. 8/2, fol. 8ʳ; Aut 8/2, fol. 37ʳ; Landsberg 8/2, p. 7.
23 Winter, 'The sketches', p. 198. Although he discusses the whole sequence of sketches, Winter was unable to determine the dating of Nottebohm's first and second musical excerpts because the sketchbook from which they are taken (Aut. 8/2) was inaccessible at the time.
24 Transcription from Nottebohm, 'Skizzen', p. 187; Winter ('The sketches', p. 197) reads a single crotchet on the third beat of bar 1. The source of this entry is Landsberg 8/1, p. 12.
25 The story has a sequel. According to Otto Jahn and Leopold Sonnleithner, Carl Czerny claimed that Beethoven said after the performance that the choral finale was a mistake, and that he would substitute an instrumental one (*Thayer's Life*, p. 895). There is no corroboration for the story, and Schindler denied it. As Thayer says, the one thing we can be sure of is that, if Beethoven did really consider this, he didn't do it.

26 Willetts, *Beethoven and England*, p. 46.
27 Schindler, *Beethoven*, pp. 271–2.
28 Quoted in ibid., p. 274.
29 Ibid., p. 282.
30 *Thayer's Life*, p. 899.
31 Quoted in H. C. Robbins Landon, *Beethoven: a Documentary Study* (abridged edn, London, 1974), p. 181.
32 *Thayer's Life*, p. 905.
33 It is sometimes stated, on the evidence of Thalberg (ibid., p. 909) that Conradin Kreutzer also directed, from the keyboard. But it seems more likely that, as Levy suggests ('Early performances', p. 45), Kreutzer's role was limited to the *Missa Solemnis* extracts.
34 This comment refers specifically to the third movement. The very extensive review in which it appears (reprinted in Levy, 'Early performances', pp. 71ff) covered both the 7 May performance and a repetition given on 23 May. For an analysis of Kanne's review, see Robin Wallace, *Beethoven's Critics: Aesthetic Dilemmas and Resolutions during the Composer's Lifetime* (Cambridge, 1986), pp. 74–7.
35 Quoted in Jacques-Gabriel Prod'homme, *Les symphonies de Beethoven* (Paris, 1906), p. 440.
36 Presumably Böhm means Umlauf. Louis Duport, who managed the Kärntnerthor Theater, trained the choir.
37 Quoted in Robbins Landon, *Beethoven*, p. 181.
38 *Thayer's Life*, p. 909.
39 Quoted in Robbins Landon, *Beethoven*, p. 182. Sonnleithner adds that Beethoven had the recitatives played 'quickly, that is, not exactly *presto* but not *andante* either'. According to Schindler, however, 'Beethoven had this recitative performed so fast that its effect was like thunder.' (Quoted in Levy, 'Early performances', p. 348).
40 Schindler, *Beethoven*, p. 283.
41 Elliott Graeme, *Beethoven: a Memoir* (London, 1874), pp. 163–4.
42 Schindler, *Beethoven*, p. 280. Thayer objects that the money from the theatre was handed over subsequently (*Thayer's Life*, p. 910), but Schindler refers to the report, not the cash.
43 Romain Rolland, *Beethoven* (London, 1921), pp. 46–7.

2 Early impressions

1 Karl-Heinz Köhler et al., *Ludwig van Beethovens Konversationshefte* (10 vols., Leipzig, 1968–), vol. 6, p. 240.
2 For a technical discussion of this, relating specifically to the second subject group, see William Caplin, 'Structural expansion in Beethoven's sonata forms', in William Kinderman (ed.), *Beethoven's Compositional Process* (Nebraska, 1991), pp. 44ff.
3 See the account of the Boldrini sketchbook, p. 4 above.
4 Ralph Vaughan Williams, *Some Thoughts on Beethoven's Choral Symphony with Writings on Other Musical Subjects* (London, 1953), p. 25.

5 This claim seems to have been first made in the *Gazette de Saint-Pétersbourg*, 16 (=28) April, 1853 (quoted in Prod'homme, *Les symphonies*, p. 468). Grove (*Beethoven*, p. 359) ridiculed the idea; by Schenker's time it had become accepted as fact (Heinrich Schenker, *Beethovens neunte Sinfonie: eine Darstellung des musikalischen Inhaltes unter fortlaufender Berücksichtigung auch des Vortrages und der Literatur* (Vienna, 1912), p. 185. A translation by John Rothgeb has recently been published; see Select Bibliography for details).

6 Quoted in Levy, 'Early performances', pp. 284ff.

7 The first explicit mentions of it that I have noticed are in an article by Henry Gauntlett in *The Musical World* in 1837 and one by Chrétien Urhan in *Le Temps* in 1838 (Levy, 'Early performances', pp. 194, 321).

8 Donald Tovey, 'Ninth Symphony in D Minor, Op. 125: its place in musical art', in *Essays in Musical Analysis* (Oxford, 1935–9), p. 115. Some years later, an article by Joseph Braunstein claimed to identify the valved-horn player in the premiere ('Scoring for the horn from Haydn to Strauss', *International Musician*, 47/10 (1949), p. 22).

9 James Webster ('The form of the finale of Beethoven's Ninth Symphony', *Beethoven Forum*, 1 (1992), pp. 25–62) gives an account of these interpretations, together with an analysis that enlarges upon some of the points made in the following paragraph. He argues that the movement is through-composed to a much greater extent than has been previously recognized.

10 Winter, 'The sketches', pp. 182ff, on which the rest of this paragraph is based. Winter's account is based principally on gathering VI of Landsberg 8/2, since the sketches in Aut. 8/1 were not available to him. But they fit well into the framework of his analysis.

11 William Kinderman has suggested that this is part of a network of religious symbolism linking the Ninth Symphony with other works, particularly the *Missa solemnis*; see his 'Beethoven's symbol for the deity in the *Missa solemnis* and Ninth Symphony' (*19th-Century Music*, 9 (1985), pp. 102–18) and 'Beethoven's compositional models for the chorale finale of the Ninth Symphony', in William Kinderman (ed.), *Beethoven's Compositional Process*, pp. 160–88.

12 See Nottebohm, *Skizzen*, pp. 189–91 (the words are translated, in a slightly different reading, in *Thayer's Life*, pp. 892–4).

13 Henry Chorley, *Music and Manners* (London; 1844), vol. 3, p. 66.

14 Letter of 1820 to William Speyer, quoted in Adam Carse, *The Orchestra from Beethoven to Berlioz* (Cambridge, 1948), p. 319.

15 Quoted in Harold Schonberg, *The Great Conductors* (London, 1968), p. 71.

16 Richard Wagner, *Prose Works*, ed. and trans. William Ashton Ellis (8 vols., London, 1898), vol. 4, pp. 306–7.

17 Willetts, *Beethoven and England*, p. 51.

18 Levy ('Early performances', p. 166) takes this to be a review of the first performance proper, but this seems unlikely in view of the reference in the next issue to this critic's comments having been 'borne out by the performance'. In this case, it is curious that the author speaks of the symphony being tried for the third time.

19 Willetts, *Beethoven and England*, p. 40.

20 Adam Carse, 'The Choral Symphony in London', *Music and Letters*, 32 (1951), p. 58.

21 The conversation books bear out Smart's account of the meeting, quoted in Willetts, *Beethoven and England*, p. 42. According to Smart, Beethoven said that, at the Vienna performances, the symphony lasted three quarters of an hour. Presumably there was a misunderstanding – although there is a story that Richard Strauss once managed to get through the symphony this fast (Schonberg, *Great Conductors*, p. 239), but he must have omitted the repeats in the second movement.

22 He described it as 'an awful work, and a perfect infliction on principals and chorus' (Edith Crashaw, 'Wagner and the Ninth Symphony', *The Musical Times*, 1 December 1925, p. 1090).

23 Carse, 'Choral Symphony', p. 54, from which the following details are also taken.

24 There is no direct evidence that Alsager, the editor, wrote the reviews. But the circumstantial evidence is strong. Moscheles described Alsager as 'a complete Beethoven fanatic' (Willetts, *Beethoven and England*, pp. 53–4), and Davison took over the music reports in 1846, the year of Alsager's death.

3 Performance and tradition

1 Daniel Koury, *Orchestral Performance Practices in the Nineteenth Century: Size, Proportions, and Seating* (Ann Arbor, 1986), p. 74.

2 Carl Bamberger (ed.), *The Conductor's Art* (New York, 1965), p. 195.

3 Richard Wagner, *My Life*, trans. Andrew Gray, ed. Mary Whittall (Cambridge, 1983), p. 57.

4 Or possibly 1840 (see the discussion in Klaus Kropfinger, *Wagner and Beethoven: Richard Wagner's Reception of Beethoven* (Cambridge, 1991), pp. 34ff).

5 Wagner, *Prose Works*, vol. 4, p. 300–303. According to Schindler, even Habeneck had problems with the instrumental recitatives, which he took much too slowly (Levy, 'Early performances', p. 348).

6 It's perhaps no coincidence that the first Leipzig performance, in 1826, had taken place at a similar benefit concert (Levy, 'Early performances', p. 357). The basic source for the Dresden performance is Wagner, *My Life*, pp. 328–33.

7 John Burk (ed.), *Letters of Richard Wagner: the Burrell Collection* (New York, 1972), p. 129.

8 Carse, 'Choral Symphony', pp. 56–7.

9 Carse, *Orchestra*, p. 357, from which the following quotations are also taken.

10 See John Warrack (ed.), *C. M. von Weber: Writings on Music* (Cambridge, 1981), p. 305. Weber is writing with specific reference to *Euryanthe*.

11 *The Letters of Beethoven*, ed. and trans. E. Anderson (London, 1961), no. 1545.

12 Quoted in Richard Taruskin, 'Beethoven symphonies: the new antiquity', *Opus*, October 1987, p. 36.

13 Quoted in Schindler, *Beethoven*, p. 409.

14 Reproduced in Richard Taruskin, 'Resisting the Ninth', *19th Century Music*, 12 (1989), p. 255.

15 Ibid., p. 254.

16 Koury, *Orchestral Performance Practices*, p. 193.

17 Geoffrey Skelton (ed.), *Cosima Wagner's Diaries* (New York, 1978), vol. 1, p. 488.

18 Heinrich Porges, *Die Afführung von Beethovens neunter Symphonie unter Richard Wagner in Bayreuth* (Leipzig, 1872).

19 Wagner, *Prose Works*, vol. 5, pp. 229–53.

20 See, for instance, Fétis's comments of 1828 in *The Harmonicon* (quoted in Schonberg, *Great Conductors*, pp. 67–8) and Gauntlett's comments of 1837 in *The Musical World* (quoted in Levy, 'Early performances', p. 198).

21 Wagner, *My Life*, p. 331; a note on p. 334 of Cosima's manuscript confirms the date.

22 Walter Damrosch, 'Hans von Bülow and the Ninth Symphony', *Musical Quarterly*, 13 (1927), p. 287.

23 Felix Weingartner, *Weingartner on Music & Conducting* (New York, 1969), p. 203.

24 This score (which is one of two in the Anna Mahler Collection, Hartley Library) is unpublished, but some transcriptions are provided in Denis McCaldin, 'Mahler and Beethoven's Ninth Symphony', *Proceedings of the Royal Musical Association*, 107 (1981), pp. 101–9; see also David Pickett, 'Gustav Mahler as an interpreter' (Ph.D. diss., University of Surrey, 1989). William McKinney, 'Gustav Mahler's score of Beethoven's Ninth Symphony: a document of orchestral performance practice in the nineteenth century' (D.M.A. diss., University of Cincinnati, 1973) gives details of a similar, but not identical, score in the archives of Universal Edition, Vienna.

25 David Wooldridge, *Conductor's World* (London, 1970), p. 194.

26 *Weingartner on Music*, p. 182.

27 McKinney, 'Gustav Mahler's Score', p. 158.

28 Grove, *Beethoven*, p. 357.

29 Prod'homme, *Les Symphonies*, p. 466.

30 Schenker, *Beethovens neunte Sinfonie*, pp. 148ff.

31 Schenker could hardly have anticipated the development of 'period' orchestras like the Hanover Band and the London Classical Players. In the Hanover Band's recording, directed by Roy Goodman (Nimbus NI 5148), the winds (which are not doubled) are perfectly audible above the strings, but they have something of the wheezy quality that Wagner disliked.

32 Schenker, *Beethovens neunte Sinfonie*, pp. 158, 154, 150; translations here and elsewhere are by Rothgeb. The last note in the upper stave of Schenker's example (on which Ex. 17 is based) is incorrect; he has C in place of D.

33 Ibid., pp. 71, 46, 49.

34 Wagner, *Prose Works*, vol. 4, pp. 314–15.

35 Peter Heyworth, *Conversations with Klemperer* (London, 1973), p. 34. In 1915, however, Schoenberg performed the work in Mahler's version; as Berg explains in a letter dated 30 March, the score and parts were borrowed from Mahler's widow, Alma (Juliane Brand, Christopher Hailey, and Donald Harris, *The Berg-Schoenberg Correspondence: Selected Letters* (London, 1982), p. 232). In a letter dated 30 April, Berg described the performance as 'incomparably beautiful', but the critics were not impressed.

36 *Weingartner on Music*, p. 63.
37 Schenker, *Beethovens neunte Sinfonie*, p. 339. Weingartner was troubled by this passage; Mahler leaves it untouched. See Appendix 2.
38 Ibid., p. 67.
39 Hellmut Federhofer, *Heinrich Schenker nach Tagebüchern und Briefen in der Oswald Jonas Memorial Collection* (Hildesheim, 1985), p. 120.
40 Currently available on EMI CDH7 69801–2. For a discography see Peter Pirie, *Furtwängler and the Art of Conducting* (London, 1980).
41 Ibid., p. 49.
42 Schonberg, *Great Conductors*, p. 272.
43 Ibid., pp. 276–7.
44 Paul Henry Lang in *The Recordings of Beethoven as Viewed by the Critics from High Fidelity* (Westport, 1971), p. 12.
45 Ibid., p. 24.
46 Spike Hughes, *The Toscanini Legacy: a Critical Study of Arturo Toscanini's Performances of Beethoven, Verdi and Other Composers* (New York, 1969), pp. 87–8.
47 Teldec 2292–46452–2 (Chamber Orchestra of Europe).
48 EMI CDC 7492212 (Norrington, London Classical Players) and Florilegium 425517–2 (Hogwood, Academy of Ancient Music). Norrington's live performances do not adhere so rigidly to the metronome markings.
49 According to Vaughan Williams, 'Beethoven was a truly religious man, and was therefore not ashamed to place earthly jollity cheek by jowl with deep adoration.' Thus the tenor soloist in the *Alla Marcia* section is a drunken soldier (probably a Welshman); the text at this point suggests that 'the stars were jolly good fellows, fond of a rousing chorus, fond of a glass of beer and a kiss from the barmaid' (*Some Thoughts*, pp. 44–5).

4 The Romantic Ninth

1 No. 378 (July–October 1896), p. 455, quoted in Elsie and Denis Arnold, 'The view of posterity: an anthology', in Denis Arnold and Nigel Fortune (eds.), *The Beethoven Companion* (London, 1971), p. 518.
2 Antony Hopkins, *The Nine Symphonies of Beethoven* (London, 1981), pp. 251–2.
3 Grove, *Beethoven*, p. 349.
4 Edwin Evans, *Beethoven's Nine Symphonies Fully Described and Analysed* (London, 1923), p. 267.
5 Tovey, 'Ninth Symphony', p. 100.
6 Basil Lam, 'Ludwig van Beethoven', in Robert Simpson (ed.), *The Symphony*, vol. 1, p. 161.
7 Robert Simpson, *Beethoven Symphonies* (London, 1970), p. 60.
8 Hopkins, *Nine Symphonies*, p. 258.
9 Leo Treitler, 'History, criticism, and Beethoven's Ninth Symphony', in *Music and the Historical Imagination* (Cambridge, 1989), pp. 23, 21.
10 Grove, *Beethoven*, p. 393. Grove was no doubt thinking of the critic in *The*

Harmonicon who expressed his 'hope that this new work of the great Beethoven may be put into a produceable form' (see p. 43 above).

11 Vol. 1 (10 July 1852), pp. 109–10.

12 See above, pp. 37–8.

13 Wallace, *Beethoven's Critics*, p. 56.

14 *Caecilia*, 8 (1828), p. 231; see Wallace, *Beethoven's Critics*, pp. 77ff, on which this paragraph is based.

15 Ernest Sanders, 'Form and content in the finale of Beethoven's Ninth Symphony', *Musical Quarterly*, 50 (1964), p. 60.

16 Wallace, *Beethoven's Critics*, pp. 83–4.

17 Wagner, *Prose Works*, vol. 7, pp. 41–2.

18 Ibid., vol. 7, pp. 251–2.

19 These notices are translated in ibid., vol. 8, pp. 201–3.

20 Quoted in Leo Schrade, *Beethoven in France: the Growth of an Idea* (New Haven, 1942), p. 194.

21 Wagner, *My Life*, pp. 384, 401, 417.

22 Wagner, *Prose Works*, vol. 8, pp. 232–8.

23 Ibid., vol. 1, p. 126.

24 Ibid., vol. 5, p. 101.

25 Koury, *Orchestral Performance Practices*, p. 193.

26 Ludwig Nohl, *Life of Beethoven* (Chicago, 1881), p. 160.

27 Details and references relating to the copying of Waldmüller's portrait may be found in Alessandra Comini, *The Changing Image of Beethoven: a Study in Mythmaking* (New York, 1987), pp. 295–7. See also Kropfinger, *Wagner and Beethoven*, pp. 1–2.

28 Schindler, *Beethoven*, p. 454.

29 See above, p. 15.

30 Comini, *Changing Image*, p. 296.

31 Wagner, *Prose Works*, vol. 5, pp. 94–5.

5 The twentieth-century Ninth

1 These translations are taken from Maynard Solomon's 'The Ninth Symphony: a search for order', in *Beethoven Essays* (Cambridge, 1988), p. 14. Solomon cites the Russian edition of Serov's analysis of the Ninth; there is also a German translation ('Die neunte Symphonie von Beethoven. Ihr Bau und ihre Idee', *Aufsätze zur Musikgeschichte* (Berlin, 1955), pp. 235–47).

2 If Réti knew of Serov and his ideas, he was not admitting it; 'to the best of my knowledge,' he writes, 'this book represents the first attempt to analyze the particular type of compositional process described in the following pages.' (Rudolph Réti, *The Thematic Process in Music* (New York, 1951), p. vii.)

3 Réti, *Thematic Process*, p. 30.

4 See my *Guide to Musical Analysis* (London, 1987), pp. 89ff.

5 Réti, *Thematic Process*, p. 275.

6 Wagner, *Prose Works*, vol. 7, p. 252. For contrasting views on the early use of this term, see Kropfinger, *Wagner and Beethoven*, pp. 114ff, and Thomas Grey, 'Richard Wagner and the aesthetics of form in the mid-nineteenth century (1840–1860)' (Ph.D. diss., Berkeley, 1988), pp. 280–1.

7 Schenker, *Beethovens neunte Sinfonie*, p. vii.

8 Ibid., p. vi.

9 Translated in Bojan Bujic (ed.), *Music in European Thought 1851–1912* (Cambridge, 1988), p. 119.

10 Schenker, *Beethovens neunte Sinfonie*, p. 245.

11 Ibid., p. 243.

12 Schenker explicitly rejects this interpretation on p. 278.

13 Schenker, *Beethovens neunte Sinfonie*, p. 247.

14 Ibid., p. 258.

15 Ibid., p. 320.

16 Martin Cooper, *Beethoven: the Last Decade* (London, 1970), p. 326.

17 Vaughan Williams, *Some Thoughts*, pp. 43–4.

18 Arnold, 'View of posterity', p. 519.

19 Berlioz's long and interesting review is translated in its entirety by Levy in 'Early performances', pp. 313–20.

20 Schumann, *On Music and Musicians*, p. 100.

21 Réti, *Thematic Process*, pp. 27ff.

22 Schenker, *Beethovens neunte Sinfonie*, p. 268.

23 Wagner, *Prose Works*, vol. 7, p. 252.

24 Joseph Kerman, *The Beethoven Quartets* (Oxford, 1967), p. 194.

25 Schenker, *Beethovens neunte Sinfonie*, pp. 268–9. Schenker also seized upon Nottebohm's argument regarding Beethoven's vacillation over the choral finale (p. 17 above); 'The time must come', he wrote, 'when Beethoven's two words "finale instromentale" will by themselves give the lie to Wagner's whole thesis!' (pp. 307–8).

26 Ibid., p. 253.

27 Leo Treitler, '"To worship that celestial sound": motives for analysis', in *Music and the Historical Imagination*, p. 62.

28 Treitler, 'History, criticism', p. 23.

29 Treitler, '"To worship"', pp. 59–60.

30 Grove, *Beethoven*, p. 349.

31 The most extensive tabulation of these is in Lionel Pike, *Beethoven, Sibelius, and the 'Profound Logic': Studies in Symphonic Analysis* (London, 1978), pp. 25–30.

32 Solomon, 'Ninth Symphony', p. 10.

33 In the *Allgemeine musikalische Zeitung*, 30 May, 1832 (Levy, 'Early performances', p. 423).

34 *Gazette de Saint-Pétersbourg*, 16 (=28) April, 1853; quoted in Prod'homme, *Les Symphonies*, p. 468.

35 Friedrich Blume, *Classic and Romantic Music: a Comprehensive Survey* (London, 1979), p. 52.

36 Cooper, *Last Decade*, p. 337.

37 Ibid., p. 330.

38 Tovey, 'Ninth Symphony', p. 125.

39 Cooper, *Last Decade*, p. 333.

40 See above, p. 39.

41 Wallace, *Beethoven's Critics*, p. 86.

42 Wagner, *Prose Works*, vol. 7, p. 253.

43 Michael Steinberg, 'Writing about Beethoven', in Winter and Carr, *Beethoven, Performers, and Critics*, p. 22.

44 Quoted in Grove, *Beethoven*, p. 392.

45 This review, published in the *Allgemeine musikalische Zeitung*, No. 52 (27 December 1826), is unsigned; the suggestion that it is by Fink is Levy's ('Early performances', p. 364).

46 Solomon, 'Ninth Symphony', p. 10.

47 Wolfgang Iser, *The Act of Reading: a Theory of Aesthetic Response* (Baltimore, 1978), p. 29.

48 Schrade, *Beethoven in France*, pp. 135–6.

49 David Levy, 'Wolfgang Robert Griepenkerl and Beethoven's Ninth Symphony', in Jerald Graue (ed.), *Essays on Music for Charles Warren Foxe* (Rochester, 1979), p. 112.

50 Maurice Kufferath, 'La neuvième Symphonie de Beethoven et l'Ode de Schiller', *L'Art musical*, 82 (1882), p. 37.

51 Note, however, the anonymous description of the Ninth Symphony as 'the grand masonic hymn of Europe' (*The Musical World*, 21 July 1837, quoted by Levy, 'Early performances', p. 205).

52 Schrade, *Beethoven in France*, p. 194.

53 Ibid., p. 243.

54 Ibid., pp. 248–9.

55 Pamela Potter, 'The Deutsche Musikgesellschaft, 1918–38', *Journal of Musicological Research*, 11 (1991), pp. 151–76; Eric Levi, personal communication.

56 'Xiyang zichanjieji yinyue dui wo de duhai' ('I was poisoned by the bourgeois music of the West'), *Guangming Ribao* (*Enlightened Daily*), 4 March 1965; see Richard Kraus, *Pianos and Politics in China: Middle-Class Ambitions and the Struggle over Western Music* (New York, 1989), p. 118.

57 'Xile de <Huan Le Song> he Beiduofen <Di Jiu Jiao Xiang Qu> de hechang yuezhan' ('Schiller's "Ode to Joy" and the choral movement of Beethoven's "Symphony No. 9"'), *Renmin Yinyue* (*People's Music*), 8 (1979), pp. 36–9.

58 Wagner, *Prose Works*, vol. 2, p. 289; Marx, *Ludwig van Beethoven: Leben und Schaffen*, translated in Ruth Solie, 'Beethoven as secular humanist: ideology and the Ninth Symphony in nineteenth-century criticism', in Eugene Narmour and Ruth Solie (eds.), *Explorations in Music, the Arts, and Ideas: Essays in Honor of Leonard B. Meyer* (Stuyvesant, 1988), p. 31.

59 For an account of this see Schrade, *Beethoven in France*, pp. 151ff.

60 Rolland, *Beethoven*, pp. 42, 15.

61 Letter of 19 October 1815 (Anderson, *Letters*, no. 63). Rolland does *not* quote the rest of the letter, which relates the remark to the tribulations of the Countess's journey from Vienna to her estate in Croatia.

62 'Shi xi Beiduofen Dijiujiaoxiangqu de yinyue neirong he sixiang qingxiang' ('An analysis of the music of Beethoven's Ninth Symphony and its philosophical content'), *Renmin Yinyue*, 11–12 (1979), pp. 72–5.

63 Yano Junichi, 'Why is Beethoven's Ninth so well loved in Japan?', *Japan Quarterly*, 12 (1982), p. 477; the exact date is not given.

64 Quoted in Yano, 'Why is', p. 477.

65 Kurisaka Yoshiro, 'A song of sympathy and gladness', *Japan Quarterly*, 12 (1982), p. 480.

66 Irene Suchy, 'The reception of Beethoven's Ninth Symphony in Japan: a case study of cultural transfer' (unpublished paper).

67 CBS Sony 32DC539.

68 Rose Rosengard Subotnik, 'Adorno's diagnosis of Beethoven's late style: early symptom of a fatal condition', *Journal of the American Musicological Society*, 29 (1976). This paragraph is based on p. 258.

69 Lisa Mary Chan, *The Huppy Handbook: Life and Times of the Young Hong Kong Professional* (Hong Kong, 1988), p. 101.

Conclusion: Beyond interpretation?

1 Anderson, *Letters*, nos. 1267, 1269, 1270.

2 William Witte, *Schiller and Burns, and Other Essays* (Oxford, 1959), pp. 34–5. The speech is *Die Tugend in ihren Folgen betrachtet*.

3 Bernt von Heiseler, *Schiller* (London, 1962), p. 91.

4 For details see Maynard Solomon, 'Beethoven and Schiller', in *Beethoven Essays* (Cambridge, 1988), pp. 205–15.

5 von Heiseler, *Schiller*, p. 92.

6 Thomas Mann, *Doctor Faustus: The Life of the German Composer Adrian Leverkühn as Told by a Friend to Thomas Mann* (London, 1949), p. 478.

7 Subotnik, 'Adorno's diagnosis', pp. 242–3.

8 Basil Deane, 'The symphonies and overtures', in Arnold and Fortune, *The Beethoven Companion*, p. 313.

9 Maynard Solomon, *Beethoven* (New York, 1977), p. 437.

10 Quoted in Schrade, *Beethoven in France*, p. 3.

11 Rey Longyear, 'Beethoven and romantic irony', in Paul Henry Lang (ed.), *The Creative World of Beethoven* (New York, 1971), pp. 149–50.

12 David Cairns and Roger Norrington; see *The Beethoven Newsletter*, 4/3 (winter, 1989), p. 61.

13 Grove, *Beethoven*, p. 385; Hopkins, *Nine Symphonies*, p. 281; Cooper, *Beethoven*, p. 340; Tovey, 'Ninth Symphony', p. 124; Treitler,'"To worship"', p. 64.

14 Köhler, *Konversationshefte*, vol. 1, p. 235.

15 Solomon, 'Ninth Symphony', p. 30.

16 Grove, *Beethoven*, p. 389.

17 Subotnik, 'Adorno's diagnosis', p. 263.

18 Steinberg, 'Writing about Beethoven', p. 23.

19 Treitler, '"To worship"', p. 56.

Select bibliography

Biography

Thayer's Life of Beethoven, rev. and ed. Elliott Forbes (2 vols., Princeton, 1967)
Solomon, Maynard, *Beethoven* (New York, 1977).

Sketches

Brandenburg, Sieghard, 'Die Skizzen zur neunten Symphonie', in *Zur Beethoven 2: Aufsätze und Dokumente*, ed. Harry Goldschmidt (Berlin, 1984), pp. 88–129
Johnson, Douglas, Alan Tyson, and Robert Winter, *The Beethoven Sketchbooks: History, Reconstruction, Inventory* (Oxford, 1985)
Winter, Robert, 'The sketches for the "Ode to Joy" ', in Robert Winter and Bruce Carr (eds.), *Beethoven, Performers, and Critics* (Detroit, 1980), pp. 176–214

Analysis

Schenker, Heinrich, *Beethovens neunte Sinfonie: eine Darstellung des musikalisches Inhaltes unter fortlaufender Berücksichtigung auch des Vortrages und der Literatur* (Vienna, 1912, second edition, 1969), trans. John Rothgeb as *Beethoven's Ninth Symphony. A portrayal of its Musical Content, with Running Commentary on Performance and Literature as Well* (New Haven, 1992)
Solomon, Maynard, 'The Ninth Symphony: a search for order', in *Beethoven Essays* (Cambridge, 1988), pp. 3–32
Tovey, Donald, 'Ninth Symphony in D Minor, Op. 125: its place in musical art' , in *Essays in Musical Analysis* (Oxford, 1935–9), vol. 2, pp. 83–127
Treitler, Leo, 'History, criticism, and Beethoven's Ninth Symphony' and ' "To worship that celestial sound": motives for analysis', in *Music and the Historical Imagination* (Cambridge, 1989), pp. 19–45, 46–66
Webster, James, 'The form of the finale of Beethoven's Ninth Symphony', *Beethoven Forum*, 1 (1992), pp. 25–62

Performance

Taruskin, Richard, 'Resisting the Ninth', *19th-Century Music*, 12 (1989), pp. 241–56
Wagner, Richard, 'The rendering of the Ninth Symphony', in *Prose Works*, ed. and trans. William Ashton Ellis (8 vols., London, 1898), vol. 5, pp. 229–53

129

Reception

Kropfinger, Klaus, *Wagner and Beethoven: Richard Wagner's Reception of Beethoven* (Cambridge, 1991)

Levy, David, 'Early performances of Beethoven's Ninth Symphony: a documentary study of five cities' (Ph.D. diss., Eastman School of Music, Rochester, 1979)

Solie, Ruth, 'Beethoven as secular humanist: ideology and the Ninth Symphony in nineteenth–century criticism', in Eugene Narmour and Ruth Solie (eds.), *Explorations in Music, the Arts, and Ideas: Essays in Honor of Leonard B. Meyer* (Stuyvesant, 1988), pp. 1–42

Wallace, Robin, *Beethoven's Critics: Aesthetic Dilemmas and Resolutions during the Composer's Lifetime* (Cambridge, 1986)

Index